INTRODUCING
ISSUES WITH
OPPOSING
VIEWPOINTS®

Civil
Liberties

Lauri S. Friedman, *Book Editor*

GREENHAVEN PRESS
A part of Gale, Cengage Learning

GALE
CENGAGE Learning™

Detroit • New York • San Francisco • New Haven, Conn • Waterville, Maine • London

Christine Nasso, *Publisher*
Elizabeth Des Chenes, *Managing Editor*

© 2010 Greenhaven Press, a part of Gale, Cengage Learning

For more information, contact:
Greenhaven Press
27500 Drake Rd.
Farmington Hills, MI 48331-3535
Or you can visit our Internet site at gale.cengage.com

For product information and technology assistance, contact us at

Gale Customer Support, 1-800-877-4253
For permission to use material from this text or product, submit all requests online at www.cengage.com/permissions

Further permissions questions can be e-mailed to permissionrequest@cengage.com

Articles in Greenhaven Press anthologies are often edited for length to meet page requirements. In addition, original titles of these works are changed to clearly present the main thesis and to explicitly indicate the author's opinion. Every effort is made to ensure that Greenhaven Press accurately reflects the original intent of the authors. Every effort has been made to trace the owners of copyrighted material.

Cover image © Valery Rizzo/Alamy.

LIBRARY OF CONGRESS CATALOGING-IN-PUBLICATION DATA
Civil liberties / Lauri S. Friedman, book editor.
p. cm. -- (Introducing issues with opposing viewpoints)
Includes bibliographical references and index.
ISBN 978-0-7377-4732-4 (hardcover)
1. Civil rights--United States. 2. National security--United States. 3. Terrorism--United States--Prevention. I. Friedman, Lauri S.
JC599.U5C5464 2010
323.0973--dc22
2009051887

Printed in the United States of America
1 2 3 4 5 6 7 14 13 12 11 10

Contents

Chapter 3: Should Limits Ever Be Placed on Free Speech?

Foreword

Indulging in a wide spectrum of ideas, beliefs, and perspectives is a critical cornerstone of democracy. After all, it is often debates over differences of opinion, such as whether to legalize abortion, how to treat prisoners, or when to enact the death penalty, that shape our society and drive it forward. Such diversity of thought is frequently regarded as the hallmark of a healthy and civilized culture. As the Reverend Clifford Schutjer of the First Congregational Church in Mansfield, Ohio, declared in a 2001 sermon, "Surrounding oneself with only like-minded people, restricting what we listen to or read only to what we find agreeable is irresponsible. Refusing to entertain doubts once we make up our minds is a subtle but deadly form of arrogance." With this advice in mind, Introducing Issues with Opposing Viewpoints books aim to open readers' minds to the critically divergent views that comprise our world's most important debates.

Introducing Issues with Opposing Viewpoints simplifies for students the enormous and often overwhelming mass of material now available via print and electronic media. Collected in every volume is an array of opinions that captures the essence of a particular controversy or topic. Introducing Issues with Opposing Viewpoints books embody the spirit of nineteenth-century journalist Charles A. Dana's axiom: "Fight for your opinions, but do not believe that they contain the whole truth, or the only truth." Absorbing such contrasting opinions teaches students to analyze the strength of an argument and compare it to its opposition. From this process readers can inform and strengthen their own opinions, or be exposed to new information that will change their minds. Introducing Issues with Opposing Viewpoints is a mosaic of different voices. The authors are statesmen, pundits, academics, journalists, corporations, and ordinary people who have felt compelled to share their experiences and ideas in a public forum. Their words have been collected from newspapers, journals, books, speeches, interviews, and the Internet, the fastest growing body of opinionated material in the world.

Introducing Issues with Opposing Viewpoints shares many of the well-known features of its critically acclaimed parent series, Opposing Viewpoints. The articles are presented in a pro/con format, allowing readers to absorb divergent perspectives side by side. Active reading questions preface each viewpoint, requiring the student to approach the material thoughtfully and carefully. Useful charts, graphs, and cartoons supplement each article. A thorough introduction provides readers with crucial background on an issue. An annotated bibliography points the reader toward articles, books, and Web sites that contain additional information on the topic. An appendix of organizations to contact contains a wide variety of charities, nonprofit organizations, political groups, and private enterprises that each hold a position on the issue at hand. Finally, a comprehensive index allows readers to locate content quickly and efficiently.

Introducing Issues with Opposing Viewpoints is also significantly different from Opposing Viewpoints. As the series title implies, its presentation will help introduce students to the concept of opposing viewpoints, and learn to use this material to aid in critical writing and debate. The series' four-color, accessible format makes the books attractive and inviting to readers of all levels. In addition, each viewpoint has been carefully edited to maximize a reader's understanding of the content. Short but thorough viewpoints capture the essence of an argument. A substantial, thought-provoking essay question placed at the end of each viewpoint asks the student to further investigate the issues raised in the viewpoint, compare and contrast two authors' arguments, or consider how one might go about forming an opinion on the topic at hand. Each viewpoint contains sidebars that include at-a-glance information and handy statistics. A Facts About section located in the back of the book further supplies students with relevant facts and figures.

Following in the tradition of the Opposing Viewpoints series, Greenhaven Press continues to provide readers with invaluable exposure to the controversial issues that shape our world. As John Stuart Mill once wrote: "The only way in which a human being can make some approach to knowing the whole of a subject is by hearing what can be said about it by persons of every variety of opinion and studying all modes in which it can be looked at by every character of mind. No wise man ever acquired his wisdom in any mode but this." It is to this principle that Introducing Issues with Opposing Viewpoints books are dedicated.

Introduction

Hundreds of years before the terrorist attacks of September 11, 2001, and the flurry of social, political, and legal changes that followed, a great American warned his fellow citizens about the difficult choices to be made when balancing their civil liberties with national security. In 1759 Benjamin Franklin said, "They that can give up essential liberty to obtain a little temporary safety deserve neither liberty nor safety." Despite this warning, the terrible threat of terrorism has in fact led many Americans to approve of giving up certain liberties in exchange for security, though their willingness to do so has decreased as more time passes since the 2001 attacks. Looking at how American attitudes about civil liberties have changed in the years since September 11 reveals much about national discourse on this important and ongoing issue.

Just nine days after the September 11 attacks, NBC News asked a wide sample of Americans how willing they would be to give up their personal freedoms and civil liberties to prevent another terrorist attack. As the site of the former Twin Towers was still smoldering, a whopping 75 percent of Americans said they were very or somewhat willing to forgo these rights and privileges to be safer from terrorism. In 2002 a *Newsweek* poll found that only 12 percent of Americans thought the government was going too far in restricting civil liberties for the sake of fighting terrorism—59 percent said the government was handling the situation just right, and 23 percent even said the government was not going far enough to restrict civil liberties. Clearly, in the immediate aftermath of the attacks, most Americans felt comfortable trading certain freedoms to feel more secure. Many, such as U.S. appeals court judge Richard A. Posner, said that the American way of life should be changed to protect against further attacks. Posner said that laws protecting civil liberties handicap the United States in its efforts to fight terrorists and are "one more sign that we do not take the threat of terrorism seriously enough to be willing to reexamine a commitment to a rather extravagant conception of civil liberties that was formed in a different and safer era."[1]

Two years after September 11, however, American opinions had slightly shifted: Although the majority of Americans still said they would be willing to sacrifice civil liberties for national security, a 2003 Associated Press poll found that 66 percent were now concerned that new antiterrorism measures would eventually restrict their freedom. As the years progressed and America experienced no new attacks, this position became more popular, and Americans' willingness to give up civil liberties in exchange for security dropped even further. Five years after the attacks, a 2006 FOX News poll revealed that 54 percent of Americans would be willing to give up some of their personal freedom to reduce the threat of terrorism. Though that number still represented the majority of Americans, it had dropped significantly since the days immediately following September 11. Another poll that year asked Americans whether they thought the government was going too far or not far enough in restricting people's civil liberties in order to fight terrorism. The results were quite different from 2002—four years later, just 34 percent thought the government had struck the right balance, and only 19 percent thought it was not going far enough. Forty-one percent said they thought the government was going too far in restricting civil liberties.

That number grew in 2006, 2007, and 2008, as stories emerged revealing that the U.S. government had used its authority to listen in on the conversations of Americans without first obtaining a warrant. Reports of immigrant harassment and racial profiling added to the disapproval, as did the erroneous placement of several popular and national figures—such as the musician formerly known as Cat Stevens and the politician Ted Kennedy—on no-fly lists. Efforts to institute a national ID card program were similarly met with skepticism and opposition. Finally, the news that American interrogators had been authorized to use torture and harsh interrogation techniques such as waterboarding on suspected terrorists led many to lose faith that their country had achieved the right balance between security and liberty.

The cumulative result of these developments left Americans feeling they had traded too much. In fact, by 2009, as President George W. Bush left office, a Gallup Poll found that 73 percent of Americans disapproved of the way civil liberties had been handled under his administration, with 35 percent saying the nation had stood still on this issue and 38 percent saying it had lost ground. A CBS News/*New York Times* poll conducted around the same time found that more Americans—51 percent—were now concerned that the government would restrict civil liberties, while only 31 percent were concerned that the government would fail to enact strong antiterrorism laws. The tide of public opinion had clearly shifted. More Americans were now more wary of what their own government might do in the name of preventing terrorism than they were about an actual terrorist attack itself. And many recalled what Senator Russell Feingold had said in 2001, when he cast the only Senate vote in opposition to the antiterrorism law known as the PATRIOT Act: "Preserving our freedom is one of the main reasons that we are now engaged in this new war on terrorism. We will lose that war without firing a shot if we sacrifice the liberties of the American people."[2]

Clearly, American ideas about the right balance between civil liberties and security have changed in the years since the September 11 attacks, and one might expect they would shift again should another horrible attack occur. Achieving the right balance between civil liberties and security is among the many issues debated in *Introducing Issues with Opposing Viewpoints: Civil Liberties*. Pro/con article pairs expose readers to the basic debates surrounding civil liberties issues— such as free speech, racial profiling, warrantless wiretapping, and protection from terrorism—and encourage them to develop their own opinions on the matter.

Notes
1. Richard A. Posner, "We Need Our Own MI5," *Washington Post*, August 15, 2006, p. A13.
2. Russell Feingold, address to the U.S. Senate, Washington, DC, October 25, 2001.

Chapter 1

What Is the State of Civil Liberties in the United States?

The September 11, 2001, terrorist attack on the World Trade Center in New York led to debate over the issue of privacy versus protecting the nation.

Americans' Civil Liberties Are Protected

George W. Bush

"The Patriot Act has not diminished American liberties; the Patriot Act has helped to defend American liberties."

Former president George W. Bush urges that the sixteen measures of the PATRIOT Act about to expire at the end of 2005 be made permanent. Bush argues that provisions in the PATRIOT Act strengthen America in four important ways. These provisions relate to information sharing between law enforcement and government agencies, to the use of the same tools that law enforcement has in fighting drug crime, to ways of combating high-tech threats from the Internet, and to the protection of American civil liberties.

George W. Bush was America's forty-third president, holding office from 2001 to 2009.

George W. Bush, "President Discusses PATRIOT Act, Ohio State Highway Patrol Academy, Columbus, Ohio," georgewbush-whitehouse.archives.gov, June 9, 2005.

AS YOU READ, CONSIDER THE FOLLOWING QUESTIONS:
1. What tool(s) used against criminals does Bush mention as helpful in the war on terror?
2. How does the PATRIOT Act help against high-tech threats involving the Internet?
3. What provisions in the PATRIOT Act protect civil liberties?

Since 2001, we've more than tripled spending on homeland security, and we've increased funding more than tenfold for the first responders who protect our homeland. Law enforcement officers stand between our people and great dangers, and we're making sure you have the tools necessary to do your job.

We've also improved our ability to track terrorists inside the United States. A vital part of that effort is called the USA Patriot Act. The Patriot Act closed dangerous gaps in America's law enforcement and intelligence capabilities—gaps the terrorists exploited when they attacked us on September the 11th [2001]. Both houses of Congress passed the Patriot Act by overwhelming bipartisan majorities—98 out of 100 United States senators voted for the act. That's what we call bipartisanship. The Patriot Act was the clear, considered response of a nation at war, and I was proud to sign that piece of legislation.

Over the past three-and-a-half years, America's law enforcement and intelligence personnel have proved that the Patriot Act works, that it was an important piece of legislation. Since September the 11th, federal terrorism investigations have resulted in charges against more than 400 suspects, and more than half of those charged have been convicted. Federal, state, and local law enforcement have used the Patriot Act to break up terror cells in New York and Oregon and Virginia and in Florida. We've prosecuted terrorist operatives and supporters in California, in Texas, in New Jersey, in Illinois, and North Carolina and Ohio. These efforts have not always made the headlines, but they've made communities safer. The Patriot Act has accomplished exactly what it was designed to do—it has protected American liberty, and saved American lives.

The problem is, at the end of this year, 16 critical provisions of the Patriot Act are scheduled to expire. Some people call these "sunset provisions." That's a good name—because letting that—those provisions expire would leave law enforcement in the dark. All 16 provisions are practical, important, and they are constitutional. Congress needs to renew them all—and this time, Congress needs to make the provisions permanent.

We need to renew the Patriot Act because it strengthens our national security in four important ways. First, we need to renew the critical provisions of the Patriot Act authorize better sharing of information between law enforcement and intelligence. Before the Patriot Act, criminal investigators were separated from intelligence officers by a legal and bureaucratic wall. A federal prosecutor who investigated Osama bin Laden in the 1990s explained the challenge this way: "We could talk to citizens, local police officers, foreign police officers—we could even talk to al Qaeda members. But there was one

Deputy assistant attorney general in the office of legal council of the U.S. Justice Department during the George W. Bush administration, John Yoo (pictured) was a strong supporter of the PATRIOT Act.

group of people we were not permitted to talk to—the FBI agents across the street from us assigned to parallel intelligence investigations of Osama Bin Laden and al Qaeda. That was a wall."

Finding our enemies in the war on terror is tough enough—law enforcement officers should not be denied vital information their own colleagues already have. The Patriot Act helped tear down this wall, and now law enforcement and intelligence officers are sharing information and working together, and bringing terrorists to justice.

In many terrorism cases, information-sharing has made the difference between success and failure—and you have an example right here in Columbus, Ohio. Two years ago, a truck driver was charged with providing support to al Qaeda. His capture came after an investigation that relied on the Patriot Act, and on contributions from more than a dozen agencies in the Southern Ohio Joint Terrorism Task Force. And members of that task force are with us today. I want to thank you for your contribution to the safety of America, and you'll understand this story I'm about to tell.

For several years, Iman Faris posed as a law-abiding resident of Columbus. But in 2000, he traveled to Afghanistan and met Osama bin Laden at an al Qaeda training camp. Faris helped the terrorists research airplanes and handle cash and purchase supplies. In 2002, he met Khalid Shaykh Muhammad—the mastermind of the September the 11th attacks—and he agreed to take part in an al Qaeda plot to destroy a New York City bridge.

After Faris returned to the United States, federal investigators used the Patriot Act to follow his trail. They used new information-sharing provisions to piece together details about his time in Afghanistan, and his plan to launch an attack on the United States. They used the Patriot Act to discover that Faris had cased possible targets in New York, and that he'd reported his findings to al Qaeda. In the spring of 2003, the FBI confronted Faris, and presented the case they had built against him. The case against him was so strong that Faris chose to cooperate, and he spent the next several weeks telling authorities about his al Qaeda association. Faris pled guilty to the charges against him. And today, instead of planning terror attacks against the American people, Iman Faris is sitting in an American prison.

The agents and prosecutors who used the Patriot Act to put Faris behind bars did superb work, and they know what a difference information-sharing made. Here is what one FBI agent said—he said, "The Faris case would not have happened without sharing information." That information-sharing was made possible by the Patriot Act. Another investigator on the case said, "We never would have had the lead to begin with." You have proved that good teamwork is critical in protecting America. For the sake of our national security, Congress must not rebuild a wall between law enforcement and intelligence.

Second, we need to renew the critical provisions of the Patriot Act that allow investigators to use the same tools against terrorists that they already use against other criminals. Before the Patriot Act, it was easier to track the phone contacts of a drug dealer than the phone contacts of an enemy operative. Before the Patriot Act, it was easier to get the credit card receipts of a tax cheat than an al Qaeda bankroller. Before the Patriot Act, agents could use wiretaps to investigate a person committing mail fraud, but not to investigate a foreign terrorist. The Patriot Act corrected all these pointless double standards—and America is safer as a result.

One tool that has been especially important to law enforcement is called a roving wiretap. Roving wiretaps allow investigators to follow suspects who frequently change their means of communications. These wiretaps must be approved by a judge, and they have been used for years to catch drug dealers and other criminals. Yet, before the Patriot Act, agents investigating terrorists had to get a separate authorization for each phone they wanted to tap. That means terrorists could elude law enforcement by simply purchasing a new cell phone. The Patriot Act fixed the problem by allowing terrorism investigators to use the same wiretaps that were already being using against drug kingpins and mob bosses. The theory here is straightforward: If we have good tools to fight street crime and fraud, law enforcement should have the same tools to fight terrorism.

Americans Are Divided on Whether Their Civil Liberties Have Been Protected

A 2006 Gallup Poll found Americans divided on whether the George W. Bush administration struck the right balance between security and liberty as it tried to protect the country from further terrorist attacks. Republicans believed the right balance had been struck; Democrats thought policies went too far.

Bush Administration Policies in Restricting Civil Liberties to Fight Terrorism

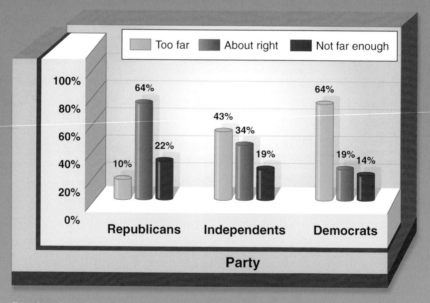

Taken from: Gallup Poll, January 6–8, 2006.

Third, we need to renew the critical provisions of the Patriot Act that updated the law to meet high-tech threats like computer espionage and cyberterrorism. Before the Patriot Act, Internet providers who notified federal authorities about threatening e-mails ran the risk of getting sued. The Patriot Act modernized the law to protect Internet companies who voluntarily disclose information to save lives.

It's common sense reform, and it's delivered results. In April 2004, a man sent an e-mail to an Islamic center in El Paso, and threatened to burn the mosque to the ground in three days. Before the Patriot Act, the FBI could have spent a week or more waiting for the information they needed. Thanks to the Patriot Act, an Internet provider was able to provide the information quickly and without fear of a lawsuit—and the FBI arrested the man before he could fulfill his—fulfill his threat.

Terrorists are using every advantage they can to inflict harm. Terrorists are using every advantage of 21st century technology, and Congress needs to ensure that our law enforcement can use that same advantage, as well.

Finally, we need to renew the critical provisions of the Patriot Act that protect our civil liberties. The Patriot Act was written with clear safeguards to ensure the law is applied fairly. The judicial branch has a strong oversight role. Law enforcement officers need a federal judge's permission to wiretap a foreign terrorist's phone, a federal judge's permission to track his calls, or a federal judge's permission to search his property. Officers must meet strict standards to use any of these tools. And these standards are fully consistent with the Constitution of the U.S.

Congress also oversees the application of the Patriot Act. Congress has recently created a federal board to ensure that the Patriot Act and other laws respect privacy and civil liberties. And I'll soon name five talented Americans to serve on that board. Attorney General [Alberto] Gonzales delivers regular reports on the Patriot Act to the House and the Senate, and the Department of Justice has answered hundreds of questions from members of Congress. One Senator, Dianne Feinstein of California, has worked with civil rights groups to monitor my administration's use of the Patriot Act. Here's what she said: "We've scrubbed the area, and I have no reported abuses." Remember that the next time you hear someone make an unfair criticism of this important, good law. The Patriot Act has not diminished American liberties; the Patriot Act has helped to defend American liberties.

Every day the men and women of law enforcement use the Patriot Act to keep America safe. It's the nature of your job that many of your most important achievements must remain secret. Americans will always be grateful for the risks you take, and for the determination you bring to this high calling. You have done your job. Now those of us in Washington have to do our job. The House and Senate are moving forward with the process to renew the Patriot Act. My message to Congress is clear: The terrorist threats against us will not expire at the end of the year, and neither should the protections of the Patriot Act.

EVALUATING THE AUTHORS' ARGUMENTS:

In this viewpoint former president George W. Bush asserts that the PATRIOT Act defends civil liberties. Compare this view with the next viewpoint by OneAmerica, which argues that the PATRIOT Act diminished the constitutional rights of American citizens and legal immigrants. Which viewpoint offers more evidence for the claims made? Support your answer with evidence from each viewpoint.

Viewpoint 2

American's Civil Liberties Are Threatened

OneAmerica

"In light of the erosion of civil liberties over the last ten years, we need to find new ways to keep this country safe without weakening our essential freedoms."

OneAmerica is an organization whose mission is to protect democracy, justice, and human rights. In the following viewpoint the authors argue that civil liberties have been eroded by several acts passed since 1996. One is the PATRIOT Act, which they say authorizes the government to harass Americans who are members of political organizations, even if those organizations are perfectly legal. The authors also claim that the PATRIOT Act threatens Americans' rights to a free press and subjects them to secret searches and phone and Internet surveillance. Another act the organization says has curbed civil liberties is the National Security Entry/Exit Registration System, which requires American immigrants from Muslim countries and North Korea to register with the government. The authors fear that these and other measures represent an erosion of civil liberties, and they warn Americans to guard against further restrictions to their rights.

AS YOU READ, CONSIDER THE FOLLOWING QUESTIONS:
1. What is the Anti-Terrorism and Effective Death Penalty Act, as described by the authors?
2. What is the National Security Agency warrantless wiretapping program, as described by the authors?
3. What is the Real ID Act, according to the authors?

I n the last ten years we have seen a steady erosion of the fundamental rights and liberties on which this country was founded, all in the name of national security. Efforts to protect the nation are best served by laws that uphold the essential rights of all. Yet, this train of failed legislation has not made our country any safer and has only diminished those very freedoms which it was supposed to protect.

Threats to Immigrants and Asylum Seekers

The foundation was laid for the wave of repressive anti-terrorism legislation which followed 9/11 with the Anti-Terrorism and Effective Death Penalty Act (AEDPA) of 1996. AEDPA limited the ability of detainees to bring habeas corpus claims challenging the terms of their detention in federal court, expanded the grounds of deportability for immigrants convicted of crimes and increased criminal penalties for immigration-related offenses.

The Illegal Immigrant Reform and Immigrant Responsibility Act of 1996 (IIRIRA) curtailed the due process rights of immigrants and asylum seekers by eliminating the right of appeal and judicial review of decisions made by the Immigration and Naturalization Service (INS) agents. IIRIRA also expanded the list of crimes defined as "aggravated felonies" that made legal permanent residents and undocumented immigrants deportable, made it more difficult to apply for asylum, and expanded the grounds for exclusion and deportation of immigrants. In the last ten years, IIRIRA has caused the detention and deportation of numerous immigrant families.

U.S. Citizens Subject to Surveillance and Arrest

In 2001, just 45 days after 9/11, Congress passed the USA PATRIOT Act severely limiting the constitutional rights of immigrants and US citizens. The Act permitted non-citizens to be jailed based on mere suspicion without charges and detained indefinitely. It broadened the definition of activities considered "deportable offenses," including defining soliciting funds for an organization that the government labels as terrorist as "engaging in terrorist activity." The PATRIOT Act also subjected lawful advocacy groups to surveillance, wiretapping, harassment, and criminal action for legal political advocacy, expanded the ability of law enforcement to conduct secret searches and engage in phone and internet surveillance, and gave law enforcement access to personal medical and financial records.

Related executive orders barred press and the public from immigration hearings of those detained after September 11th, allowed the government to monitor communications between federal detainees and their lawyers, and ordered military commissions to be set up to try suspected terrorists who are not citizens. Provisions of the original law expired at the end of 2005, but Congress temporarily extended the expiration date twice, then passed a new version of the act in

Many Americans have grown increasingly concerned over the PATRIOT Act's impact on their civil liberties.

March of 2006, making permanent all but two of the Patriot Act's original provisions.

A Secret Eavesdropping Program and More

A few weeks prior to the passage of the PATRIOT Act President [George W.] Bush issued an executive order that authorized the infamous National Security Agency (NSA) warrantless wiretapping program. This secret eavesdropping program allowed the surveillance of certain telephone calls placed between a party in the United States and a party in a foreign country without obtaining a warrant through the Foreign Intelligence Surveillance Court.

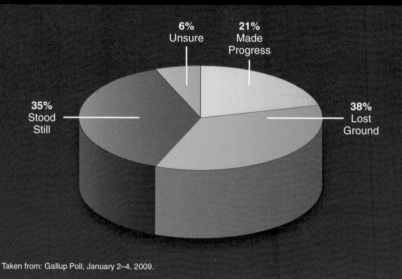

Americans Have Lost Ground on Civil Liberties

A 2009 Gallup Poll revealed that the majority of Americans—73 percent—believe the United States has either stood still or lost ground on civil liberties since 2000.

"Do you think civil liberties in the United States have made progress, stood still or lost ground since George W. Bush became president?"

6%
Unsure

21%
Made
Progress

35%
Stood
Still

38%
Lost
Ground

Taken from: Gallup Poll, January 2–4, 2009.

In August of 2002 the Department of Justice initiated the National Security Entry/Exit Registration System (NSEERS) "special registration" program requiring nearly 85,000 men from 24 Muslim countries and North Korea to voluntarily report to INS facilities for "special registration" which entailed finger-printing, photographing, and questioning about their immigration status. The men were required to appear for annual interviews if they stayed in the US for more than one year and to register with immigration officials when they leave the country. While no terrorist has been found through the program 13,000 of the men who voluntarily reported ended up in deportation proceedings due to their immigration status. In December 2003, the NSEERS program was supplemented by US-VISIT, a program that takes biometric measurements of people entering the US from certain countries, including fingerprints and face scans.

> **FAST FACT**
>
> A 2009 Gallup Poll found that 73 percent of Americans disapproved of the way civil liberties were handled under the George W. Bush administration, with 35 percent saying the nation stood still on this issue and 38 percent saying it lost ground.

Military Commissions and Real ID

In 2005 the Real ID Act was passed as an attachment to a supplemental appropriations bill for military expenses in Iraq and Afghanistan. Real ID requires people to verify legal residence in the US in order to get a driver's license, permits secret deportation hearings and trials, reduces judicial review of deportation orders and makes non-citizens (including long-time permanent residents) deportable for past lawful speech or associations.

In October of 2006 The Military Commissions Act was signed into law, effectively creating a separate system of justice for non-citizens. The act denies non-citizens the right to challenge their detention in court, allows any non-citizen to be tried by military commission and permits indefinite detention of non-citizens. The act will also allow non-citizens to be convicted on the basis of coerced testimony, hearsay evidence and warrantless searches, and sanction interrogation practices that amount to torture.

In light of the erosion of civil liberties over the last ten years, we need to find new ways to keep this country safe without weakening our essential freedoms. We maintain hope that change is possible as we work together for liberty and justice for all.

EVALUATING THE AUTHORS' ARGUMENTS:

OneAmerica thinks that once civil liberties are taken away, it is nearly impossible to get them back. How do you think George W. Bush, author of the previous viewpoint, would respond to this claim? Quote his text in your answer.

Viewpoint

3

Muslim and Arab Americans' Civil Liberties Are Routinely Violated

"Discrimination against Muslims in the post-9/11 era has taken on many forms."

Heena Musabji and
Christina Abraham

In the following viewpoint Heena Musabji and Christina Abraham argue that Muslim and Arab Americans have had their civil liberties violated ever since the September 11, 2001, terrorist attacks. Even though the vast majority of Muslim and Arab Americans are upstanding citizens, the authors say they have been treated with suspicion, detained, harassed, and persecuted just because of the way they look or the way their names are spelled. Muslims have been pulled off planes because they make people uncomfortable, and they have been denied access to flights, even though they are innocent of any wrongdoing. They have also been unfairly targeted by law enforcement officials for questioning and searches. Musabji and Abraham warn that if the civil liberties of

Heena Musabji and Christina Abraham, "The Threat to Civil Liberties and Its Effect on Muslims in America," *DePaul Journal for Social Justice*, vol. 1, Fall 2007, pp. 83–84, 91–92, 94–95, 97, 99–101, 112. Reproduced by permission.

just some groups are violated, all Americans are in jeopardy of eventually losing their rights and freedoms.

Musabji and Abraham work for CAIR-Chicago, a branch of the national organization Council on American-Islamic Relations, which advocates for Muslim and Arab rights.

AS YOU READ, CONSIDER THE FOLLOWING QUESTIONS:
1. What does the phrase "traveling while Muslim" mean in the context of the viewpoint?
2. Who is Akif Rahman, and how does he factor into the authors' argument?
3. To what kinds of interviews are Muslim and Arab Americans asked to submit, according to the authors?

The September 11, 2001 attacks on the World Trade Center changed America in many ways. The aftermath of the attacks led to vast changes in our governmental structure through the creation of The Department of Homeland Security (DHS) and the enactment of the Uniting and Strengthening America by Providing Appropriate Tools Required to Intercept and Obstruct Terrorism Act of 2001 (PATRIOT Act) and other laws and policies.

Section 102 of the PATRIOT Act condemns discrimination against Arab and Muslim Americans; yet, implementation of policies under the Act and other current U.S. policies has the opposite effect. The Act instead creates a disparate impact on individuals including denying civil rights and liberties to all people. National security is an important concern for each and every American, but as a nation we cannot sacrifice civil liberties and promote discrimination against certain groups in pursuit of such security. Such discriminatory policies can only breed a greater threat. . . .

Muslims Are Harassed While Traveling

The United States Supreme Court has stated that, "distinctions between citizens solely because of their ancestry are by their very nature odious to free people whose institutions are founded upon the doctrine of equality." Unfortunately, we find ourselves in an atmosphere where present policies create such distinctions. Racial profiling is deemed acceptable as long as it is done to protect national security. All American citizens and residents are willing to do their part to ensure their safety and the safety of others while traveling; however, all too often there are burdens that come with traveling while Muslim or looking Muslim. One of these burdens is the uncertainty of whether one can travel without substantial delay or if the ability to travel will be denied altogether. This delay or loss of mobility can result in real economic or social harms to individuals who rely on their ability to travel. The scenarios range from being removed from an airplane because an individual "looks suspicious" (a.k.a. looks Muslim) to being stopped at the border, escorted by armed officers, handcuffed, physically abused, questioned and detained because the individual was mistakenly identified as someone on a government watch list. . . .

Innocent Americans Should Not Be Treated Like Terrorists

In addition to being misidentified through a watch list, Muslims are also victims of in-person racial profiling and assumed to be threatening because of their appearance, mere physical characteristics or behavior. Being a Muslim means to be a follower of the faith of Islam, but all too often looking Muslim is wrongfully and automatically translated as being a potential terror threat. The government should not allow its policies to treat innocent Americans as terrorists.

Shortly after September 2001, a U.S. citizen of Middle Eastern origin had cleared airport security checks and boarded a United Airlines flight from Los Angeles to New York. Shortly after he was seated on the airplane he was told that his presence on the plane made the crew uncomfortable. . . .

The Case of Akif Rahman

In June 2005, the American Civil Liberties Union (ACLU) filed a lawsuit on behalf of Akif Rahman, a U.S. citizen by birth. Prior to the filing of the suit, Rahman had been unlawfully detained and questioned by DHS on five separate occasions when he re-entered the country after being abroad because he was misidentified. Four of the five detentions

In June 2005 the American Civil Liberties Union filed a lawsuit on behalf of U.S. citizen Akif Rahman (pictured), arguing that he was a victim of discrimination and harassment because he was a Muslim.

lasted anywhere from two to six hours, which is more time than necessary to determine his identity for re-entry into the United States. On May 8, 2005, Rahman entered the United States after a trip with his family to Canada through the Detroit-Windsor tunnel. After presenting his identification he was told by the DHS officer to turn off his vehicle, hand over his keys and was escorted by agents away from his family. He was detained for six hours, handcuffed for three of them and kicked while they searched his person. His wife and two young children were detained separately for six hours with no food. It is a travesty for an innocent individual and his family to be detained for six hours to clear up an issue of misidentification.

On June 19, 2006, the ACLU amended the Rahman complaint to add other similarly situated plaintiffs to the class action [lawsuit]. The named plaintiffs are all U.S. citizens of South Asian or Middle Eastern descent and almost all are Muslim. They all travel regularly for lawful reasons such as business and family trips. None of the named plaintiffs have engaged in any unlawful conduct that would provide justification for mistreatment to them or their families upon re-entering their country of citizenship. . . .

The PATRIOT Act Is Used Against Arabs and Muslims

Although the PATRIOT Act was renewed with some modifications to the provisions that caused the greatest amount of criticism among the public, the Act still raises concerns over the preservation of civil liberties in the United States. Although the Act does not explicitly target Arabs or Muslims as a group, it is clear that its effect is most strongly felt by Arab and Muslim Americans. . . .

One of the ways in which law enforcement officers use the USA PATRIOT Act to target Arab and Muslim Americans is by asking them to submit to "voluntary interviews." Indeed, these interviews are voluntary, but sometimes the individual is not made aware of this fact. Often, the individual is not made aware of his or her rights to have an attorney present. On occasion, the individual is told he or she "does not need an attorney." Usually, such a comment is enough to intimidate the individual into submitting to the interview without attorney representation. CAIR-Chicago has seen many of these cases firsthand. . . .

> ## FAST FACT
>
> According to an assessment of Muslim and Arab rights by the Council on American-Islamic Relations, the number of profiling incidents experienced by these groups increased 340 percent from 2006 to 2007.

What is important to note is that the PATRIOT Act has not merely lowered the standard for allowing law enforcement officers to search and seize the property of others, but it has also extended the ability of law enforcement to seek out and question suspects. Since the agent knows nothing of the individual going into the interview, there is no

Civil Rights Violations: Complaints of Arab and Muslim Americans

Each year the Council on American–Islamic Relations (CAIR) receives more complaints about civil rights violations of Arabs and Muslims. In 2007, most of these were related to profiling, due process, religious issues, employment, hate mail, and immigration issues.

Total Number of Civil Rights Complaints by Year

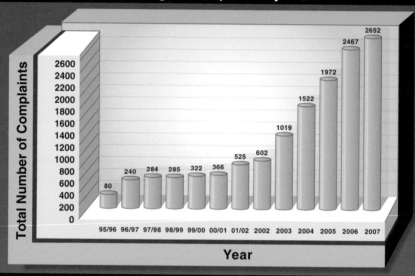

Number of Complaints by Type of Alleged Abuse, 2007

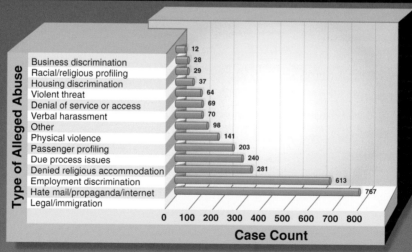

Taken from: Council on American–Islamic Relations, *The Status of Muslim Civil Rights in the United States 2008: Without Fear or Discrimination.*

basis for suspecting the person of having committed a crime. All that is generally known about the individual is that he or she is Arab and/or Muslim and that he or she may have espoused criticism about the U.S. policies or know of someone who has. Because the interviews are ultimately voluntary, the law enforcement officer has crossed no line legally. Although the agent's actions are not illegal, the intimidation tactics that are sometimes used to get people to submit to such interviews and the initial motivation for the interview based on the person's ethnicity or religion is contrary to the principles of the constitution. . . .

Everyone's Rights Must Be Protected

Religious discrimination against Muslims in the post-9/11 era has taken on many forms. . . . Such discrimination has manifested in restricting the Muslims right to travel, restricting the rights of inmates and denying due process rights to the accused. These forms affect some of the most fundamental values of American society. At the heart of these values is the idea that government does not bestow rights upon individuals, individuals are born with these rights and for this reason are always entitled to them. Therefore, it becomes incumbent on all members of society to collectively fight for the rights to which all members of society are entitled. Society has a civic duty to protect the rights guaranteed to all of its members. This is the only way that society can build a system of support whereby the rights of all are ultimately protected.

EVALUATING THE AUTHORS' ARGUMENTS:

Heena Musabji and Christina Abraham warn that protecting the rights of "some" is the only way to protect the rights of "all." What do you think they mean by this? In three or four sentences, flesh out this idea. Then state whether you agree.

Reports of Muslim and Arab Americans' Civil Liberties Violations Are Exaggerated

Steven Emerson

"CAIR [the Council on American-Islamic Relations] considers law enforcement investigations involving Muslims to be anti-Muslim acts."

In the following viewpoint Steven Emerson argues that reports that Muslim and Arab Americans have had their civil liberties violated usually turn out to be exaggerated or phony. He criticizes the Council on American-Islamic Relations (CAIR) for pushing an image of Muslim and Arab Americans as victims. Emerson says CAIR encourages people to file reports about events that in reality are very minor, but this practice leads to false or exaggerated claims of abuse. Furthermore, Emerson says that although CAIR complains that Muslim and Arab Americans have been questioned about terrorism, law enforcement investigations involving Muslims are not necessarily anti-Muslim—most often they are warranted, given the nature of the war on terror. Emerson urges people not to believe

Steven Emerson, "CAIR's Hate Crimes," *The Investigative Project on Terrorism,* 2008. Copyright © 2008 The Investigative Project on Terrorism. Reproduced by permission.

CAIR's claims that Muslim and Arab Americans have had their rights systematically violated.

Emerson is a journalist who writes about national security, terrorism, and Islamic extremism.

AS YOU READ, CONSIDER THE FOLLOWING QUESTIONS:
1. According to Emerson, what does CAIR hope to muster opposition to?
2. What did articles in the *Weekly Standard* and the *Washington Times* say about CAIR, as reported by the author?
3. Who is Mirza Akram, and how does he factor into the author's argument?

C AIR [the Council on American-Islamic Relations] has created a niche for itself in the American-Muslim community by documenting what it perceives as anti-Muslim incidents, challenging the "stereotyping" of Muslims and connections between Islam and terrorism on grounds that these depictions make Muslims vulnerable to harassment and hate crimes. As Executive Director Nihad Awad wrote in his 2003 testimony before a U.S. Senate panel, "there has . . . been an astonishing increase in the volume of anti-Muslim rhetoric in the media and politics today."

Incidents Involving Muslims Are Not Anti-Muslim
Each year, CAIR bemoans the "anti-Muslim hysteria" that has turned Muslim-Americans into "second-class citizens." For example, in its 2004 report, *"The Status of Muslim Civil Rights in the United States 2004: Unpatriotic Acts,"* CAIR states, "Last year marked the highest number of Muslim civil rights cases ever recorded by CAIR's annual report. . . . Reports of harassment, violence, and discriminatory treatment increased nearly 70 percent over 2002."

But CAIR considers law enforcement investigations involving Muslims to be anti-Muslim acts. It has repeatedly included such investigations in its annual report on alleged civil rights abuses and discrimination against Muslims. . . .

Turning Muslims into Victims

More generally, the [organization] tries to persuade American citizens that government policy has resulted in an undeserved backlash against ordinary Muslims. By doing so, CAIR hopes to muster opposition to the anti-terror laws it finds objectionable. A June 2003 *US News and World Report* column elaborates on CAIR's motives:

> Why do CAIR and other groups push the "bias" button so hard? Well, the victim stance works. It attracts press attention and has made the "bias against Muslims" article a staple of big-city dailies. It encourages Muslims to feel angry and non-Muslims to feel guilty. It raises a great deal of money, garners a lot of TV time, and gets the attention of Congress. And by pre-positioning all future criticism as bias, it tends to intimidate or silence even the most sensible critics. From a lobbying point of view, who would want to give up a set of advantages like this?

Phony Data and Exaggerated Incidents

As *US News and World Report* indicates, there are serious problems with CAIR's claims of a "growing Islamophobic prejudice." *The Weekly Standard* blasted CAIR after it released its 2004 report for its "shoddy information gathering" and "its politicized interpretation of the 'data.'" The article added that CAIR "clearly has an axe to grind," that it relies entirely on self-reporting, and that it makes "molehills become mountains." *The Washington Times* notes that CAIR "unashamedly exaggerates the number of such incidents" and that "the data is phony."

Responding to CAIR's 2003 report, the Justice Department called the group's claims irresponsible: "We're talking about unfair criticism based on a lot of misinformation and propaganda," a department spokesman said.

CAIR allows people to file complaints online, or download the complaint form and mail it in with optional supporting documents, such as photos and police reports. The group urges the complainant to file a report, "even if you believe it is a 'small' incident."

Undermining the FBI

According to the FBI, CAIR purposefully ignores the request of its agents to keep quiet about ongoing investigations.

The Council on American-Islamic Relations (CAIR), led by executive director Nihad Awad (pictured), is highly critical of civil liberties violations against Muslims. However, the author points to several news organizations, as well as the FBI, that characterize CAIR's stance as being inaccurate and politicized.

Ross Rice, a spokesman for the Chicago FBI, cited the 2005 case of a local Muslim family who received telephone death threats from an unidentified individual. The FBI was investigating the complaint and the caller, if found, could face felony charges, Rice said.

Rice told the *Chicago Tribune* that the FBI had asked CAIR not to publicize the case. But CAIR issued a release anyway, which drew local media coverage. By failing to heed the FBI's wishes, he said, CAIR "compromised or impeded our investigation." . . .

Crimes Against Muslims Are Not Necessarily Hate Crimes

On July 9, 2004, a fire caused $50,000 in damage at the Continental Spices Cash & Carry, a Pakistani-owned grocery store in Everett, Washington, specializing in Pakistani, Indian and Middle Eastern foods. After putting out the fire, Everett police and firefighters found a gasoline can and a derogatory message directed toward Arabs spray-painted on a wall. A white cross was spray-painted on a refrigerator in the back of the store.

Police cautioned against hastily labeling the incident a hate crime. The department spokesman, Sgt. Boyd Bryant, said, "We need to give the detectives time to do their job."

Rejecting that advice, CAIR issued a press release the following day that "called on local and national leaders to address the issue of growing Islamophobic prejudice following an arson attack on a Muslim-owned business in Washington State."

But on August 19, police arrested the store's owner, Mirza Akram, on a federal arson warrant. He was accused of setting fire to the store to collect insurance on the building and its contents. The U.S. attorney alleged that mounting financial losses led Akram to stage the arson and then make it look like a hate crime.

> **FAST FACT**
>
> According to a 2007 study conducted by the Council on American-Islamic Relations, reports of anti-Muslim hate crimes decreased by 19 percent, while incidents involving the police decreased by 42 percent.

Civil Liberties Will Improve Under the Obama Administration

Barack Obama

"[We] cannot keep this country safe unless we enlist the power of our most fundamental values . . . freedom, fairness, equality, and dignity."

Barack Obama is the forty-fourth president of the United States. In the following viewpoint he lays out the steps his administration is taking to reverse injustices that he says occurred under the administration of his predecessor George W. Bush. Obama explains he is making it illegal to use harsh interrogation techniques that were previously used on suspected terrorists. These were illegal in the international community's eyes, and Obama says they only helped rally terrorists around the idea that America is worthy of being attacked. He also promises that unlawful prisons will be closed and the government will keep fewer secrets from the American people. Obama believes that a nation cannot be secure unless it is free, and he says that true freedom and security will be achieved only when the United States bases its security policies on its most fundamental values of liberty and justice for all.

Barack Obama, "Remarks by the President on National Security," in www.whitehouse.gov, May 21, 2009.

AS YOU READ, CONSIDER THE FOLLOWING QUESTIONS:
1. What does Obama say serves as a recruitment tool for terrorists?
2. In what way has the prison at Guantánamo Bay weakened national security, according to Obama?
3. What is the "state secrets" privilege, and what changes to it does Obama propose?

These are extraordinary times for our country. We're confronting a historic economic crisis. We're fighting two wars. We face a range of challenges that will define the way that Americans will live in the 21st century. So there's no shortage of work to be done, or responsibilities to bear. . . .

In the midst of all these challenges, however, my single most important responsibility as President is to keep the American people safe. It's the first thing that I think about when I wake up in the morning. It's the last thing that I think about when I go to sleep at night. . . .

But I believe with every fiber of my being that in the long run we also cannot keep this country safe unless we enlist the power of our most fundamental values. The documents that we hold in this very hall—the Declaration of Independence, the Constitution, the Bill of Rights—these are not simply words written into aging parchment. They are the foundation of liberty and justice in this country, and a light that shines for all who seek freedom, fairness, equality, and dignity around the world. . . .

The Previous Administration Traded Liberty for Security

Unfortunately, faced with an uncertain threat, our government made a series of hasty decisions. I believe that many of these decisions were motivated by a sincere desire to protect the American people. But I also believe that all too often our government made decisions based on fear rather than foresight; that all too often our government trimmed facts and evidence to fit ideological predispositions. Instead of strategically applying our power and our principles, too often we set those principles aside as luxuries that we could no longer afford.

Should the Bush Administration Be Investigated?

The majority of Americans want members of the Bush Administration to be investigated for violating civil liberties during their time in office.

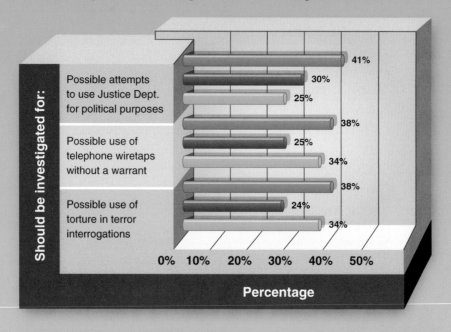

Should be investigated for:

Possible attempts to use Justice Dept. for political purposes
- 41%
- 30%
- 25%

Possible use of telephone wiretaps without a warrant
- 38%
- 25%
- 34%

Possible use of torture in terror interrogations
- 38%
- 24%
- 34%

Percentage scale: 0% 10% 20% 30% 40% 50%

Percentage

Preferred Action on Bush Administration Policies/Actions

- Criminal Investigation
- Investigation by Independent panel
- Neither

Taken from: *USA Today*/Gallup Poll, January 30– February 1, 2009.

And during this season of fear, too many of us—Democrats and Republicans, politicians, journalists, and citizens—fell silent.

In other words, we went off course. . . .

Now let me be clear: We are indeed at war with al Qaeda and its affiliates. We do need to update our institutions to deal with this threat. But we must do so with an abiding confidence in the rule of law and due process; in checks and balances and accountability. For reasons that I will explain, the decisions that were made over the last eight years established an ad hoc legal approach for fighting terrorism that was neither effective nor sustainable—a framework that failed to rely on our legal traditions and time-tested institutions, and that failed to use our values as a compass. And that's why I took several steps upon taking office to better protect the American people.

Harsh Interrogation Techniques Are No Longer Allowed

First, I banned the use of so-called enhanced interrogation techniques by the United States of America.

I know some have argued that brutal methods like waterboarding were necessary to keep us safe. I could not disagree more. As Commander-in-Chief, I see the intelligence. I bear the responsibility for keeping this country safe. And I categorically reject the assertion that these are the most effective means of interrogation. What's more, they undermine the rule of law. They alienate us in the world. They serve as a recruitment tool for terrorists, and increase the will of our enemies to fight us, while decreasing the will of others to work with America. They risk the lives of our troops by making it less likely that others will surrender to them in battle, and more likely that Americans will be mistreated if they are captured. In short, they did not advance our war and counterterrorism efforts—they undermined them, and that is why I ended them once and for all.

Now, I should add, the arguments against these techniques did not originate from my administration. As Senator [John] McCain once said, torture "serves as a great propaganda tool for those who recruit people to fight against us." And even under President [George W.] Bush, there was recognition among members of his own administration—including a Secretary of State, other senior officials, and many in the military and intelligence community—that those who argued for these tactics were on the wrong side of the debate, and the wrong side of history. That's why we must leave these methods where they belong—in the past. They are not who we are, and they are not America.

Unlawful Prisons Will Be Closed

The second decision that I made was to order the closing of the prison camp at Guantánamo Bay.

For over seven years, we have detained hundreds of people at Guantánamo. During that time, the system of military commissions that were in place at Guantánamo succeeded in convicting a grand total of three suspected terrorists. Let me repeat that: three convictions in over seven years. Instead of bringing terrorists to justice, efforts at prosecution met setback after setback, cases lingered on, and in 2006 the Supreme Court invalidated the entire system. Meanwhile, over 525 detainees were released from Guantánamo under not my administration, under the previous administration. Let me repeat that: Two-thirds of the detainees were released before I took office and ordered the closure of Guantánamo.

There is also no question that Guantánamo set back the moral authority that is America's strongest currency in the world. Instead of building a durable framework for the struggle against al Qaeda that drew upon our deeply held values and traditions, our government was defending positions that undermined the rule of law. In fact, part of the rationale for establishing Guantánamo in the first place was the misplaced notion that a prison there would be beyond the law—a proposition that the Supreme Court soundly rejected. Meanwhile, instead of serving as a tool to counter terrorism, Guantánamo became a symbol that helped

In a May 2009 speech in Washington, D.C., President Barack Obama discusses his intention to change controversial national security policies implemented by the George W. Bush administration.

al Qaeda recruit terrorists to its cause. Indeed, the existence of Guantánamo likely created more terrorists around the world than it ever detained.

So the record is clear: Rather than keeping us safer, the prison at Guantánamo has weakened American national security. It is a rallying cry for our enemies. It sets back the willingness of our allies to work with us in fighting an enemy that operates in scores of countries. By any measure, the costs of keeping it open far exceed the complications involved in closing it. That's why I argued that it should be closed throughout my campaign, and that is why I ordered it closed within one year. . . .

No More Unnecessary State Secrets

Now, along these same lines, my administration is also confronting challenges to what is known as the "state secrets" privilege. This is a doctrine that allows the government to challenge legal cases involving secret programs. It's been used by many past Presidents—Republican and Democrat—for many decades. And while this principle is absolutely necessary in some circumstances to

protect national security, I am concerned that it has been over-used. It is also currently the subject of a wide range of lawsuits. So let me lay out some principles here. We must not protect information merely because it reveals the violation of a law or embarrassment to the government. And that's why my administration is nearing completion of a thorough review of this practice.

And we plan to embrace several principles for reform. We will apply a stricter legal test to material that can be protected under the state secrets privilege. We will not assert the privilege in court without first following our own formal process, including review by a Justice Department committee and the personal approval of the Attorney

General. And each year we will voluntarily report to Congress when we have invoked the privilege and why because, as I said before, there must be proper oversight over our actions.

On all these matters related to the disclosure of sensitive information, I wish I could say that there was some simple formula out there to be had. There is not. These often involve tough calls, involve competing concerns, and they require a surgical approach. But the common thread that runs through all of my decisions is simple: We will safeguard what we must to protect the American people, but we will also ensure the accountability and oversight that is the hallmark of our constitutional system. . . .

Toward a Freer and Safer America

Now, in all the areas that I've discussed today, the policies that I've proposed represent a new direction from the last eight years. To protect the American people and our values, we've banned enhanced interrogation techniques. We are closing the prison at Guantánamo. We are reforming military commissions, and we will pursue a new legal regime to detain terrorists. We are declassifying more information and embracing more oversight of our actions, and we're narrowing our use of the state secrets privilege. These are dramatic changes that will put our approach to national security on a surer, safer, and more sustainable footing. Their implementation will take time, but they will get done.

> ## EVALUATING THE AUTHORS' ARGUMENTS:
>
> Barack Obama explains the ways in which civil liberties have improved or will improve under his presidency. How would Ivan Eland, author of the following viewpoint, respond to this claim? Use evidence from both texts in your answer.

Civil Liberties Will Not Improve Under the Obama Administration

Ivan Eland

"So much for a more open government."

In the following viewpoint Ivan Eland argues that President Barack Obama has not reversed many of the most important civil liberties violations of the George W. Bush presidency. Eland admits Obama has made some important changes but says these are largely symbolic. In reality, the Obama administration plans to continue to secretly hold enemy combatants, hold prisoners indefinitely without trial, and misuse the government privilege of state secrets. On techniques and actions that Obama has outlawed, Eland says it is easy enough to reactivate these should Obama want to. For all of these reasons, Eland concludes that civil liberties under the Obama administration are not expected to be much different than they were under the George W. Bush administration.

Eland is a senior fellow at the Independent Institute, an organization that promotes nonpartisan public policy research and debate.

AS YOU READ, CONSIDER THE FOLLOWING QUESTIONS:
  1. What does the phrase "Bush Lite" mean in the context of the viewpoint?
  2. What does Eland consider to be a "symbolic act"?
  3. Who is Elena Kagan and how does she factor into the author's argument?

Barack Obama entered the presidency as one of the most rhetorically pro–civil liberties politicians in recent memory. And shortly after taking office, he drew applause from friends of liberty for promulgating executive orders closing Guantánamo and CIA [Central Intelligence Agency] secret prisons, ending CIA torture, suspending kangaroo [court] proceedings at military tribunals, and pledging more openness than the secretive Bush administration. Unfortunately, instead of prosecuting Bush administration officials, including George W. Bush, for violating criminal statutes against torture, illegal wiretapping of Americans, and other misdeeds—thus avoiding the bad precedent of giving a president a free pass on illegal acts—Obama appears ready to vindicate the prior administration's anti-terrorism program by adopting Bush Lite.

Civil Liberties Continue to Be Violated

Warning signs that Obama was softer on civil liberties than advertised came even before he took office, when as a Senator, he voted for blatantly unconstitutional legislation that allowed federal snooping into some e-mail messages and phone calls without a warrant. The Constitution implies that all government searches and seizures of private property require a judicially-approved warrant based on probable cause that a crime has been committed—with no exceptions mentioned, including for national security.

Politicians love symbolic acts and Obama's rapid pledge to shutter the high profile prison at Guantánamo and secret CIA prisons was widely praised. But if civil liberties continue to be violated elsewhere, have we made much progress?

Continuing Controversial Policies

Obama's nominees have said the administration will continue the CIA's policy of "extraordinary rendition" of terrorism suspects—a euphemism for secret kidnapping without the legal nicety of extradition or any other procedural due process rights. Prior to the Bush administration, such government-sanctioned kidnapping was authorized only to return the suspects to their home countries. The Bush administration began using such renditions to abduct suspects and send them to third-party nations that practiced harsh torture—presumably to keep U.S. hands (relatively) clean. Leon Panetta, Obama's CIA director, has said that the new administration will continue the Bush administration's practice of rendition to third party countries and relying on those countries' suspect diplomatic promises not to torture.

Also, Obama supposedly banned CIA torture by executive order, but such orders are not laws and can be reversed with the stroke of a pen. What's worse, although CIA director Panetta has admitted that water boarding (simulated drowning) is torture, he has also asserted publicly that if regular interrogation techniques did not produce information from a prisoner suspected of being involved in an imminent attack, he would request the authority to use harsher methods.

> # FAST FACT
>
> Eighty-three percent of members of the Bill of Rights Defense Committee gave the Obama administration a grade of "F" for failing to restore immediately many of the civil liberties compromised after 9/11.

Keeping Its Options Open

In perhaps the most important of the civil liberties waffling, Elena Kagan, the administration's nominee for solicitor general at the Justice Department, pledged to continue detaining indefinitely prisoners without trial, even if they were noncombatant terrorist financiers arrested far from a combat zone. Ominously, the Obama administration is stalling on taking a position on the even more important Bush-era policy of perpetually incarcerating "enemy combatants" without trial on U.S. territory. To stay within the U.S. Constitution, such vital habeas

During her nomination hearings for solicitor general, Elena Kagan (pictured) alarmed civil libertarians by commenting that the Obama administration would continue former president George W. Bush's policy of holding prisoners indefinitely without trial.

corpus rights [which are designed to prevent unlawful imprisonment], one of the pillars of the rule of law, should only be suspended by Congress in areas where combat has rendered the civilian courts inoperable —hardly the case in the United States during the never-ending "war on terror."

Although Obama's executive order suspended the Bush administration's kangaroo military tribunals, which have insufficient legal procedural safeguards, it has kept its options open on their resumption.

Finally, the new administration has mimicked the Bush administration's use of the "state secrets" doctrine to try to nix lawsuits by former CIA detainees and, for the same reason, pressured another country's court not to release information about U.S. torture of a prisoner. Traditionally, the doctrine was usually used to withhold specific evidence in a legal proceeding, not to nix entire cases against the government for malfeasance. So much for a more open government.

The New Boss Resembles the Old Boss

The Obama administration is new and should be given a chance to do the right thing. Although certainly better than the lawless Bush administration, the new boss unsurprisingly resembles the old boss.

Historically, party label has been a less good indicator about actual presidential policies than the era in which the chief executive served. For example, in terms of actual programs, Richard Nixon was the last liberal president, a chief executive who largely continued Lyndon Johnson's government penetration into American society and even further expanded it. Similarly, Jimmy Carter started the move back to the right and Ronald Reagan continued it (but in practice he really wasn't all that conservative). Civil liberties follow the general trend. After the first Word Trade Center bombing in 1993 and the Oklahoma City and Tokyo subway attacks in 1995, Bill Clinton signed the Antiterrorism and Effective Death Penalty Act of 1996, which augmented the government's powers of surveillance on Americans and paved the way for the further vast expansion of such authority (and other aforementioned dramatic civil liberties violations of the Bush administration) after 9/11.

Typically in American history, any crisis—such as 9/11—causes an expansion of government power. After the crisis recedes, a public reaction to government excesses usually ensues—as now exists with Bush policies. Yet government power never quite recedes to its precrisis level. Unfortunately, what we are likely to see from a post-9/11 Obama presidency is that same historical phenomenon playing out.

Chapter 2

How Should Civil Liberties Be Handled During the War on Terror?

The U.S. base in Guantánamo, Cuba, where suspected terrorists are housed, has been the subject of controversy in the war on terror.

Americans Must Give Up Some of Their Civil Liberties to Stay Safe

Kim Taipale

"Privacy expectations that deny government access to information that they need to prevent catastrophic terrorist attacks [are] unreasonable."

If Americans want to be safe, they must be willing to give up at least some of their liberties, argues Kim Taipale in the following viewpoint, taken from a 2007 debate about privacy and national security. Taipale explains it is very easy for terrorists to move about in a free and private society like the United States. The freedoms and civil protections afforded regular citizens—like the right to privacy—are also taken advantage of by terrorists who seek to conceal their plots. Since technology has made it easier than ever for terrorists to evade government surveillance, Taipale thinks Americans need to grant the government more power to access all types of information. Given the threat of terrorist attack, Taipale says the government needs expanded powers if it is to keep citizens safe. He concludes it is unreasonable for Americans to want total and complete privacy during a time of war.

Taipale is a lawyer and the executive director of the Center for Advanced Studies in Science and Technology Policy.

AS YOU READ, CONSIDER THE FOLLOWING QUESTIONS:
1. What does the word "sanctuary" mean in the context of the viewpoint?
2. Why, according to Taipale, did al Qaeda members choose to communicate at the New York Public Library?
3. What, according to Taipale, is not a balancing act?

I think we all agree that privacy expectations, that maintaining privacy expectations that deny government access to information that they need to prevent catastrophic terrorist attacks is unreasonable under any standard.

The question really is: What are the actions that government can take and how are those actions going to be reasonable and how are they going to be oversighted in a way that we can all feel comfortable that these constitutional principles . . . are respected.

Absolute Privacy Is Not Realistic When Fighting Terrorists

I would make three points with respect to thinking about reasonableness and oversight. First, the changing nature of the threat—the fact is that we face potentially catastrophic outcomes, and when we face the potentially catastrophic outcomes, for instance nuclear terrorism, you really do have to take a preemptive approach. You have to prevent terrorists from attacking.

Second, the technology has changed some basic assumptions about what information is available and whether that information is useful in that test. And third, that actually expectations of privacy that don't take into account those two points are inherently unreasonable.

They are unreasonable when they deny access to government arbitrarily to information that is available.

Government Agencies Must Have Enough Power to Do Their Job

For example, I point to the wall, the famous wall that separated intelligence and criminal investigations prior to 9/11. Two and a half weeks before 9/11, an FBI agent in the Intelligence Division in New York City had the names of two of the 9/11 hijackers. He asked for help from the Criminal Division to use their resources to track those two, those two who existed in San Diego and were in the phone book. He didn't have the San Diego phone book. He asked the Criminal Division to help him with that endeavor and was told by the Washington headquarters that he could not talk to the Criminal Division.

He sent an e-mail back to them saying that this decision will cost lives and I hope we can live with that in the future.

Information Cannot Be Off Limits

We also can't take a position to create sanctuaries where, for instance, we apply special rules that make certain information off limits—information that exists, again. I mean, we have to have rules about how to access it, but we can't turn it off limits. The move to try to make library records exempt from, for instance, the normal business records requirement would create a sanctuary.

There was a terrorist trial in New York City [in which a terrorist] pled guilty to material support of terrorism and said, specifically, that he went to the New York Public Library to communicate with Al Qaida members abroad, because he knew that the New York Public Library scrubbed the hard disks every night to avoid keeping records.

We can't have those kinds of information sanctuaries. We can think about what's reasonable and what kind of constraints to put on government before they access that information, but to just put it off limits is unreasonable.

Information Needs to Be Accessible to Be Useful

Secondly, privacy expectations are unreasonable when they don't take into account that the fourth amendment is not an absolute requirement for a warrant before accessing any information.

We need to have a mechanism that allows programmatic approaches to certain kinds of information access, based on reasonable suspicion,

A young woman uses a computer at the New York Public Library to access the Internet. The viewpoint author contends that library policies that protect privacy made it easy for terrorists to use library computers to plot attacks against the U.S.

based on other standards that we use every day, on the street, when police officers observe activity, use a standard of reasonable suspicion, use that to work their way up to probable cause.

. . . This is not a balancing act. The very metaphor of balance is a misnomer because it implies that somehow there's a fulcrum point at which point the exact amount of privacy and security are available.

They're not dichotomous rivals to be traded one for another. They're dual obligations, and they're dual obligations that need to be addressed and delivered subject to the constraints of the other. And that's different. That's calculus, not arithmetic.

Important Dates: Civil Liberties and National Security Since September 11, 2001

2001

September 11: Terrorists attack the World Trade Center and Pentagon.

October 26: The USA PATRIOT Act of 2001 is signed into law by President George W. Bush.

November 13: President Bush authorizes the use of military commissions to try terrorist suspects.

November 19: The Transportation Security Administration (TSA) is created, and the use of the Computer Assisted Passenger Prescreening System II (CAPPS II) to profile and assess the risk of domestic passengers is put into effect.

2002

January 11: The Department of Justice reveals that more than 710 individuals were arrested in connection with immigration violations and 108 were held on criminal charges following September 11.

February 7: According to a presidential order issued by President Bush, al Qaeda and Taliban detainees do not qualify for protections under the Geneva Conventions.

November 25: The Department of Homeland Security is established.

2003

July 3: President Bush says that for the first time since World War II, six suspected al Qaeda terrorists are eligible to stand trial before military tribunals.

September 24: The Terrorism Information Awareness Program and the Information Awareness Office are shut down.

2004

January: The government launches US-VISIT, a biometric screening process of foreign visitors.

June 28: The Supreme Court rules in *Rasul v. Bush* that Guantánamo Bay detainees are entitled to argue their claims in U.S. federal courts.

July 16: The CAPPS II passenger prescreening program is dismantled

August 26: The TSA announces that a passenger prescreening program called Secure Flight will replace CAPPSII.

August 27: The National Counterterrorism Center is established to analyze counterterrorism functions and data.

2005

May 11: The Real ID Act is signed into law. It creates nationwide standards for state identification cards and driver's licenses.

October 5: The Detainee Treatment Act is signed into law. It prohibits the torture and cruel, inhuman, or degrading treatment of prisoners but does not grant them habeas corpus rights.

November 2: The *Washington Post* reports that the CIA has established secret prisons in third-party countries. Here, high-level terrorist suspects are incarcerated and interrogated.

December 14: NBC reports that the Department of Defense has been collecting data on antiwar and other activist groups.

December 16: The *New York Times* reports that the National Security Agency has been using wiretaps to monitor telephone and e-mail communications.

2006

March 9: The USA PATRIOT Improvement and Reauthorization Act of 2005 is signed into law.

August 17: In the case of *ACLU v. NSA*, the Terrorist Surveillance Program is ruled unconstitutional under the First and Fourth Amendments.

September 6: President Bush acknowledges the existence of secret CIA prisons abroad and the CIA's use of "alternative" interrogation methods.

2007

March 21: The Justice Department reports that the FBI may have violated National Security Letter (NSL) regulations as many as three thousand times since 2003.

2008

February 5: The CIA acknowledges that at least three high-level al Qaeda suspects were subjected to waterboarding, considered by some to be torture.

September 12: The Department of Justice releases new guidelines for FBI investigations, which allow criminal investigation tactics to be used to investigate national security and foreign intelligence threats.

2009

January 22: President Barack Obama reverses Bush administration detention and interrogation policies.

Taken from: Daniel B. Prieto, "War About Terror: Civil Liberties and National Security After 9/11," Council on Foreign Relations, February 2009.

Surveillance Is Needed to Preempt Threats

The changing nature of the threat, you know, you can't deny that there's the potential for catastrophic outcomes. That requires preemption. And preemption by definition requires some form of surveillance. Preemption is based on making some judgment about the future and what's going to happen. You can't do that without observing current behavior or past behavior and making some judgment. That's what we do.

There's another problem—that we have rules that are based on this line of the border. . . . In moving to preemption, we have had this line historically between . . . domestic and foreign intelligence. . . . And the rules changed at the border.

Well, that doesn't work against an enemy who moves easily across that border and who hides among civilian populations, who moves within regular migration flows to mask their activity.

FAST FACT

An April 2009 Gallup Poll revealed that 55 percent of Americans believe that waterboarding—a technique in which a person is forced underwater for periods of time—is acceptable when used to interrogate suspected terrorists.

The Mythology of Privacy

The nature of the information availability has changed. The death of practical obscurity. . . . The economics of information means that more data is going to be available. And automated analysis and data-mining, quite frankly, means that it's more useful, that actually accessing this information can give us knowledge, can help us prevent, help us anticipate future actions.

And you know, I would just comment that some of these expectations are unreasonable in this context if they're not rethought. We live in this mythology of privacy that has a fetish for secrecy of procedural protections—the opposition to the privacy lobby, for instance, the data retention laws.

We need oversight and accountability and we need reasonableness and we need to figure out how those things are going to happen in this new environment.

Americans Do Not Have to Give Up Their Civil Liberties to Stay Safe

"Security and privacy are not opposite ends of a seesaw; you don't have to accept less of one to get more of the other."

Bruce Schneier

In the following viewpoint Bruce Schneier argues that privacy and liberty are not mutually exclusive. He says the government does not need to curtail freedom in order to provide security—many effective security measures have nothing to do with freedom, and those that curtail freedom are often ineffective. For example, he says the three elements that have made air travel safer since the September 11 attacks—cockpit door locks, the use of sky marshals, and heightened awareness of passengers—have not infringed in any way on liberty. On the other hand, security watch lists, data mining, and other measures that invade citizens' privacy have not had any measurable effect on security. Schneier warns that those who would trade liberty for security are likely to end up with neither.

Schneier is the author of *Beyond Fear: Thinking Sensibly About Security in an Uncertain World.*

AS YOU READ, CONSIDER THE FOLLOWING QUESTIONS:
1. What point does the author make about security in the former East Germany and in modern-day China?
2. What does Schneier say about the national security cases in which the government claims antiprivacy measures have helped it thwart a terror attack?
3. What, in Schneier's opinion, does liberty require?

If there's a debate that sums up post-9/11 politics, it's security versus privacy. Which is more important? How much privacy are you willing to give up for security? Can we even afford privacy in this age of insecurity? Security versus privacy: It's the battle of the century, or at least its first decade.

In a Jan. 21 *New Yorker* article, Director of National Intelligence Michael McConnell discusses a proposed plan to monitor all—that's right, *all*—internet communications for security purposes, an idea so extreme that the word "Orwellian" feels too mild.

The article (not online) contains this passage:

> In order for cyberspace to be policed, internet activity will have to be closely monitored. Ed Giorgio, who is working with McConnell on the plan, said that would mean giving the government the authority to examine the content of any e-mail, file transfer or Web search. "Google has records that could help in a cyber-investigation," he said. Giorgio warned me, "We have a saying in this business: 'Privacy and security are a zero-sum game.'"

I'm sure they have that saying in their business. And it's precisely why, when people in their business are in charge of government, it becomes a police state. If privacy and security really were a zero-sum game, we would have seen mass immigration into the former East Germany and modern-day China. While it's true that police states like those have less street crime, no one argues that their citizens are fundamentally more secure.

We've been told we have to trade off security and privacy so often —in debates on security versus privacy, writing contests, polls, reasoned essays and political rhetoric—that most of us don't even question the fundamental dichotomy.

Since 9/11, security measures such as reinforcing cockpit doors have made air travel safer without violating civil liberties.

But it's a false one.

Security and privacy are not opposite ends of a seesaw; you don't have to accept less of one to get more of the other. Think of a door lock, a burglar alarm and a tall fence. Think of guns, anti-counterfeiting measures on currency and that dumb liquid ban at airports. Security affects privacy only when it's based on identity, and there are limitations to that sort of approach.

Since 9/11, two—or maybe three—things have potentially improved airline security: reinforcing the cockpit doors, passengers realizing they have to fight back and—possibly—sky marshals. Everything else—all the security measures that affect privacy—is just security theater and a waste of effort.

By the same token, many of the anti-privacy "security" measures we're seeing—national ID cards, warrantless eavesdropping, massive data mining and so on—do little to improve, and in some cases harm, security. And government claims of their success are either wrong, or against fake threats.

The debate isn't security versus privacy. It's liberty versus control. You can see it in comments by government officials: "Privacy no longer can mean anonymity," says Donald Kerr, principal deputy director of national intelligence. "Instead, it should mean that government and businesses properly safeguard people's private communications and financial information." Did you catch that? You're expected to give up control of your privacy to others, who—presumably—get to decide how much of it you deserve. That's what loss of liberty looks like.

Americans Do Not Want to Trade Liberty for Security

Polls taken in 2006 and again in 2008 showed that Americans are increasingly more concerned that the government will pass laws restricting their civil liberties than they are that the government will fail to pass strong antiterrorism laws.

"Which concerns you more right now: that the government will fail to enact strong antiterrorism laws, or that the government will enact new antiterrorism laws which excessively restrict the average person's civil liberties?"

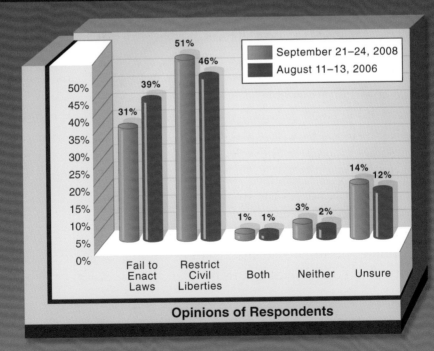

September 21–24, 2008
August 11–13, 2006

	Fail to Enact Laws	Restrict Civil Liberties	Both	Neither	Unsure
September 21–24, 2008	31%	51%	1%	3%	14%
August 11–13, 2006	39%	46%	1%	2%	12%

Opinions of Respondents

Taken from: CBS News/*New York Times* poll, September 21–24, 2008.

It should be no surprise that people choose security over privacy: 51 to 29 percent in a recent poll. Even if you don't subscribe to Maslow's hierarchy of needs, it's obvious that security is more important. Security is vital to survival, not just of people but of every living thing. Privacy is unique to humans, but it's a social need. It's vital to personal dignity, to family life, to society—to what makes us uniquely human—but not to survival.

If you set up the false dichotomy, of course people will choose security over privacy—especially if you scare them first. But it's still a false dichotomy. There is no security without privacy. And liberty requires both security and privacy. The famous quote attributed to Benjamin Franklin reads: "Those who would give up essential liberty to purchase a little temporary safety, deserve neither liberty nor safety." It's also true that those who would give up privacy for security are likely to end up with neither.

EVALUATING THE AUTHORS' ARGUMENTS:

Bruce Schneier and Kim Taipale, author of the previous viewpoint, disagree on whether it is necessary to give up freedom to enjoy a secure society. After reading both viewpoints, what are your thoughts on the matter? Do you think Americans must trade freedom for security, or can both be achieved? Cite evidence from the texts in your answer.

Viewpoint

3

Americans Should Support Warrantless Wiretaps

Mortimer B. Zuckerman

"Bin Laden himself could have made a telephone call from Waziristan to Singapore and . . . we would not have been able to listen without prior permission."

In the following viewpoint Mortimer B. Zuckerman argues that Americans should support the government's use of warrantless wiretaps. These are wiretaps that allow law enforcement officials to listen in on phone conversations without getting an official warrant to do so. Zuckerman says that even though these wiretaps are an invasion of privacy, they can help catch terrorists, who make overseas calls to accomplices in other countries. Making it easier for officials to use wiretaps will help them catch more suspected terrorists and thus reduce the probability that Americans will die in terrorist attacks. Zuckerman concludes that warrantless wiretapping is a reasonable security measure, given the nature of the terrorist enemy.

Zuckerman is editor in chief of *U.S. News & World Report*, in which this viewpoint was originally published.

AS YOU READ, CONSIDER THE FOLLOWING QUESTIONS:
  1. According to the author, what did *USA Today* compare the Bush administration to?
  2. How much potential intelligence does the author say was lost due to the need to obtain wiretap warrants?
  3. What does Zuckerman say needs to be done if a country "can't find the needle"? What does he mean by this?

How does any civilized nation cope with fanatical barbarism? What kind of people will plot to murder thousands—so crazed with hate they will kill their own families for the cause? Even after 9/11 we have been slow to recognize the nature of the beast we face. It is hard for us to comprehend the mentality of, say, the group of 21 homegrown suicidal jihadists apprehended last year in Britain. We now know not only that they were prepared to blow up 10 civilian airliners flying from London to the United States—which might have killed as many as 3,500 innocent people—but also that they planned to avoid airport scrutiny by traveling with their wives and children and were thus prepared to execute their nearest and dearest.

As a free society, we are remarkably vulnerable. Our open borders permit second-generation terrorists from Europe to infiltrate under the legal visa waiver program. We admit many imams from Egypt and Pakistan trained in Saudi Arabia under the extremist perversion of Islam known as Wahhabism. The consequences of our tolerance are spelled out in a recent report by the New York City Police Counterterrorism Department. It focuses on how difficult it is to follow the "trajectory of radicalization"—the behavior and whereabouts of homegrown radical Islamists. That New York report has to be read with the most recent National Intelligence Estimate that the external threat from al Qaeda has not waned despite expanded worldwide counterterrorism efforts.

This is the context in which to consider the protests about tightening electronic surveillance, led by the liberal *New York Times* and the ultraliberal *New Yorker* and espoused by Democrats who watered down the recent reform legislation—including an insistence that it be reviewed in six months. How far should security concerns impinge on privacy? The administration says the balance has to be recalibrated. The trouble is that the administration has lost much of its moral authority. As *USA Today* put it, the White House "has all the credibility of a teenager who has squandered his allowance and is demanding more money."

True—but on this issue, it has a real case.

Until the law was changed, bin Laden himself could have made a telephone call from Waziristan to Singapore and, if it were carried on a fiber optic cable that passes through the United States (as are the vast majority of long-distance calls), we would not have been able to listen without prior permission from the Foreign Intelligence Surveillance Act court. FISA had to approve all interceptions of foreign-to-foreign communications coming through American wires, fiber optic cables, and switching stations. With warrants to the FISA court backed up, as much as two thirds of potential intelligence from U.S. eavesdropping capabilities was being lost. The director of national intelligence, Adm. Mike McConnell, gave Congress specific examples, such as one involving the capture of three American soldiers in Iraq.

Broader reach. Congress was right to eliminate the restrictions. Warrantless wiretaps will no longer be limited to "known foreign terrorists"

Director of National Intelligence Mike McConnell provides Congress with examples of intelligence that was lost because the FISA courts were too slow to initiate wiretaps.

Americans think it is not too likely or not at all likely that the government has used warrantless wiretapping to listen in on their conversations.

"How likely is it that the federal government has ever wiretapped any of your telephone conversations: very likely, somewhat likely, not too likely, or not at all likely?"

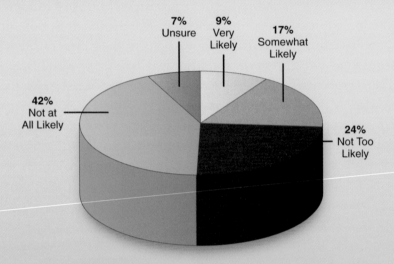

7%
Unsure

9%
Very
Likely

17%
Somewhat
Likely

42%
Not at
All Likely

24%
Not Too
Likely

Taken from: CNN poll conducted by Opinion Research Corporation, May 16–17, 2006.

but will include surveillance of the larger universe of "foreign targets," including America's enemies who are state actors and others not linked directly to al Qaeda, on the theory that if you can't find the needle, you have to examine the haystack.

Many of the Democrats supported the warrantless listening because they feared the political consequences of a terrorist attack occurring while they were on summer vacation—and because they had not taken the lead to plug the electronic intelligence gap. The Democrats have been politically vulnerable on national security and counterterrorism going back to the days of Jimmy Carter, who was so naive about the intentions of the Soviet Union when it invaded Afghanistan. (And Carter is still willing to accommodate some of the most hostile enemies of the United States.)

Even now, Democrats are focusing on the scariest possible interpretation of the new law, ignoring its well-crafted rules to protect Americans. In addition to putting in the six-month expiration, they have failed to provide liability protection to U.S. telecommunication companies. Some of these have stopped cooperating with the National Security Agency since the program was exposed.

The Democrats should think again. Their concerns for American liberty are commendable, but if there is a serious terrorist attack, the outcry from the American public will force any government to enforce security measures that transform our way of life. We must have a bipartisan policy. The president would do well to work with leaders of Congress to agree jointly on an independent body to monitor the procedures. We have distinguished retired leaders who could do this. To allow essential security to become just a point of contention will only damage the country and the American people

> **FAST FACT**
>
> A February 2009 national survey conducted by the Pew Research Center for the People & the Press found that 50 percent of Americans believe it is acceptable for the government to monitor the e-mails and telephone calls of suspected terrorists without the permission of the courts.

EVALUATING THE AUTHOR'S ARGUMENTS:

Mortimer B. Zuckerman thinks that countries with an open society like the United States are naturally prone to terrorist attacks. Give a few examples of what you think he means. In what ways does America's open society make it vulnerable to those who want to hurt it? What specific aspects of American society make it easy for terrorists to operate inside of it?

Warrantless Wiretaps Violate Civil Liberties

Patrick Radden Keefe

"The key instrument imposed by the Founders to preserve basic liberty— warrants— is something that we must now abolish."

In the following viewpoint Patrick Radden Keefe argues that warrantless wiretaps violate civil liberties. He explains that even though surveillance targets are supposed to be limited to foreign terrorists, warrantless wiretapping makes the conversations of innocent Americans available to government surveillance. Even though Keefe says this program is a violation of America's laws, it has been prevented from being labeled criminal because the facts of the program have been deemed too secret to be laid out in court. In Keefe's opinion, anything that secret is probably bad for the American people. He warns that when there is no oversight on government activities, American citizens tend to lose their freedoms. For these reasons, Keefe says Americans should be suspicious of warrantless wiretapping programs.

Keefe is the author of *The Snakehead: An Epic Tale of the Chinatown Underworld and the American Dream.*

AS YOU READ, CONSIDER THE FOLLOWING QUESTIONS:
  1. Why, according to Keefe, was a plan proposed by House Democrats to intercept communications rebuffed?
  2. Who is Senator Kit Bond, and how does he factor into the author's argument?
  3. What does Keefe say is the "bitter joke" of the proposed surveillance legislation?

S ometime today [June 25, 2008], the Senate is likely to approve the most comprehensive overhaul of American surveillance law since the Watergate era. Unless you're a government lawyer, a legal scholar, a masochist, or an insomniac, chances are you haven't read the 114-page bill. Don't beat yourself up: Neither have most of the 293 House members who voted for it last week. Ditto the mainstream press, who seem to have relied chiefly on summaries provided by the same lawmakers who hadn't read it.

A Program So Secret We Don't Really Know What It Is
To be fair, wiretapping is so classified, and the language of the bill so opaque, that no one without a "top secret" clearance can say with any authority just how much surveillance the proposal will authorize the government to do. (The best assessment yet comes from former Justice Department official David Kris, who deems the legislation "so intricate" that it risks confusing even "the government officials who must apply it.")

Out of the echo chamber of ignorance and self-serving political cant, a number of myths have begun to emerge. We may never know for sure everything that this new legislation entails. But here are a few things that it most certainly doesn't. . . .

Doing Away with Oversight
One frequent refrain in favor of the new legislation is that without it, America's intelligence capabilities will dry up, leaving the country vulnerable to attack. The National Security Agency [NSA] wants to intercept communications that pass through routers in the United States, even when both parties to the communication are abroad. The

[George W. Bush] administration has argued that the NSA should not have to obtain a court order to intercept those communications. Seems reasonable, right?

Of course it's reasonable. So reasonable, in fact, that House Democrats proposed to fix the problem a year ago. They were rebuffed. Why? Because their plan contained too much judicial oversight. (They ended up folding, just as they have this time around.) So when people say that this legislation is all about exempting foreign-to-foreign communications that happen to pass through the United States from the warrant requirement, don't buy it.

Abolishing a Basic Liberty

You see, the new law goes *a lot* further, basically doing away with warrants altogether in the domestic-to-international context. Under the proposal, the NSA can engage in what David Kris calls "vacuum cleaner surveillance" of phone calls and e-mails entering and leaving the United States through our nation's telecom switches. Provided that the "target" of the surveillance is reasonably believed to be abroad, the NSA can intercept a massive volume of communications, which might, however incidentally, include yours. When authorities want to target purely domestic communications, they still have to apply for a warrant from the [Foreign Intelligence Surveillance Act] FISA court (albeit only after a weeklong grace period of warrantless surveillance). But where communications between the United States and another country are concerned, the secret court is relegated to a vestigial role, consulted on the soundness of the "targeting procedures," but not on the legitimacy of the targets themselves.

This is a huge departure from FISA. As [writer] Glenn Greenwald argues in *Salon*, the underlying suggestion of the new proposal is "not that the FISA law is obsolete, but rather, that the key instrument im-

> **FAST FACT**
>
> According to a 2009 *Wired* magazine article, a massive data-mining operation by the FBI's National Security Branch Analysis Center has led to the collection of 1.5 billion public and private records of American citizens.

posed by the Founders to preserve basic liberty—warrants—is something that we must now abolish."

Do What the Government Tells You to Do

Perhaps most controversially, the bill effectively pardons the telecom giants that assisted the Bush administration in the warrantless wiretapping program. They will now be shielded from dozens of civil lawsuits brought against them after their involvement was exposed. House

Republican senator Kit Bond (pictured) supports the government's action that, in essence, pardoned large telecom corporations that assisted the Bush administration in implementing warrantless wiretaps.

Americans Disapprove of Warrantless Wiretapping

A CNN poll found that a slim majority of Americans think it was wrong of the George W. Bush administration to listen to overseas phone conversations between U.S. citizens and foreigners without obtaining a warrant first.

"Do you think the Bush administration was right or wrong in wiretapping telephone conversations between U.S. citizens living in the United States and suspected terrorists living in other countries without obtaining a court order?"

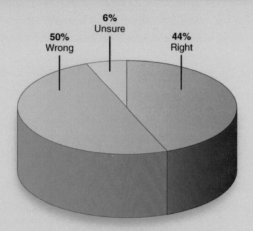

6%
Unsure

50%
Wrong

44%
Right

Taken from: CNN poll conducted by Opinion Research Corporation, May 16–17, 2006.

Democrats insist that the telecoms are not *automatically* getting off the hook. Instead, the companies must go before a federal judge. But here's the catch: For the suits against them to be "promptly dismissed," they must demonstrate to the judge not that what they did was legal but only that the White House told them to do it.

This is another bit of face-saving window dressing, and its essence is best captured in a breathtaking remark from Sen. [Kit] Bond: "I'm not here to say that the government is always right. But when the government tells you to do something, I'm sure you would all agree . . . that is something you need to do." That more or less sums it up. . . .

A Criminal Law That Cannot Be Tried in Court
Here, then, is the bitter joke of the new legislation: From 2001 to 2007, the NSA engaged in a secret program that was a straightforward violation of America's wiretapping laws. Since the program was

revealed, the administration has succeeded in preventing the judiciary from making a definitive declaration that the wiretapping was a crime. Suits against the government get dismissed on state-secrets grounds, because while the program may have been illegal, it was also so highly classified that its legality can never be litigated in open court. And now suits against the telecoms will be dismissed en masse as well. Meanwhile, the new law moves the goal posts, taking illegal things the administration was doing and making them legal.

Whatever [Maryland representative Steny] Hoyer and [House Speaker Nancy] Pelosi—and even [Barack] Obama—say, this amounts to a retroactive blessing of the illegal program, and historically it means that the country will probably be deprived of any rigorous assessment of what precisely the administration did between 2001 and 2007. No judge will have an opportunity to call the president's willful violation of a federal statute a crime, and no landmark ruling by the courts can serve as a warning for future generations about government excesses in dangerous times. What's more, because the proposal so completely plays into the Bush conception of executive power, it renders meaningless any of its own provisions. After all, if the main lesson of the wiretapping scandal is that we need more surveillance power for the government, what is to stop President Bush—or President Obama . . . —from one day choosing to set this new law aside, too? "How will we be judged?" Sen. Chris Dodd, D-Conn., asked in a stirring speech deploring the legislation yesterday. "The technical argument obscures the defining question: the rule of law, or the rule of men?"

> **EVALUATING THE AUTHOR'S ARGUMENTS:**
>
> Patrick Radden Keefe quotes from several sources to support the points he makes in his essay. Make a list of all the people he quotes, including their credentials and the nature of their comments. Then pick the quote you found most persuasive. Why did you choose it? What did it lend to Keefe's argument?

Racial Profiling Should Be Used to Catch Terrorists

Rogier van Bakel

"Suspicion falls more easily on Muslims because Muslims have turned out to be responsible for one major terrorist act after another."

Racial profiling is a commonsense way to catch terrorists, argues Rogier van Bakel in the following viewpoint. He asserts that terrorists are not a random collection of people from all different cultures—they overwhelmingly tend to be young, Muslim, and from the Middle East or Southeast Asia. Therefore, in van Bakel's opinion, it makes sense to focus on these groups of people when trying to catch terrorists. Van Bakel says that Muslims should understand why they are profiled and direct their anger not against law enforcement officials but toward the members of their community who have forced others to view them suspiciously. Van Bakel concludes that even though racial profiling is not politically correct, all Americans should admit that it is an excellent way to keep them safe.

Van Bakel is a journalist whose work has appeared in the *New York Times, Rolling*

Rogier van Bakel, "The Case for Ethnic Profiling," Nobody'sBusiness.com, August 18, 2006. Reproduced by permission of the author. www.bakelblog.com

Stone, *Wired*, the *Christian Science Monitor*, and *Reason* magazine. He writes a blog called Nobody's Business.

AS YOU READ, CONSIDER THE FOLLOWING QUESTIONS:
1. What four countries does van Bakel say terrorists are most likely to come from?
2. What, according to van Bakel, are Americans supposed to pretend about grandmothers and teenage spelling bee contestants?
3. What does van Bakel think about non-Muslim terrorists like Timothy McVeigh or Richard Reid?

I read this *Salon* piece about catching terrorism suspects. It's called "Why Racial Profiling Doesn't Work."

Racial profiling doesn't work? Bullbeef and twaddle. I would argue that—while profiling is hardly a magic bullet that will neutralize any and all terror threats—it's one of the most useful things we can do if we are serious about nabbing terrorist evildoers before they strike.

Terrorists Share a Certain Set of Qualities

No mincing words now: What, pray tell, are the most common characteristics of the terrorists who seek to inflict mass casualties on western populations? Who was behind the World Trade Center massacre, the Madrid blasts, the Bali bloodbath, the London subway bombings, and [the July 2006] foiled plot to blow up a dozen airliners over the Atlantic?

For starters, and most importantly, the perpetrators were all Muslims. In most cases, they or their parents hail from countries like Pakistan, Yemen, Indonesia and Saudi Arabia, and it follows that their names are more likely to be Tariq or Mohammed than Charlie or Franz. The vast majority of them are men, and they're mostly in their twenties and thirties.

Ignoring the Obvious—at Our Own Expense

We know this, but we're not supposed to act on it. In the United States at least, when it comes to screening for terrorists, we're supposed to pretend that a 70-year-old grandmother from Boise and a

"Spot the Suicide Bomber," cartoon by Glenn Foden. Copyright © Glenn Foden. Reproduction rights obtainable from www.CartoonStock.com.

13-year-old spelling-bee contestant from Duluth are just as likely to cause murder and mayhem as a 23-year-old engineering student who just flew in from Islamabad.

It's a dangerous and self-defeating deceit.

Unfortunately, the term "ethnic profiling"—a.k.a. "racial profiling" —is a discussion-stopper, a sure-fire way to get the *bien pensants*[1] (including the boo-hiss PC crowd) on one's side. But some form of ethnic profiling happens to be a necessity when it comes to preventing the next 9/11. Why *wouldn't* we do it? The *Salon* article offers several reasons, and every one of them is flawed.

There Are Exceptions, but There Is Still a "Rule"

Argument One: Not every terrorist fits the profile. [Oklahoma City bomber] Timothy McVeigh was a white, non-Muslim American. Richard Reid, the shoe bomber, is a British citizen with Jamaican blood.

True, but incomplete. McVeigh was an anomaly; despite supposedly like-minded small fry like Eric Rudolph, McVeigh's brand of violent rad-

---

1. A French term meaning "those who hold conventional views."

icalism has not served as an inspiration to other Americans, much less inspired a movement. As for Reid, he's not as much an exception as opponents of profiling make him out to be. Reid had begun calling himself Abdul Raheem Abu Ibrahim; he learned Arabic and dressed in traditional Islamic garb; he attended a London mosque known for its radical preachings; intelligence connected him to Al Qaeda, based in part on Reid's trip to the Khalden terrorist training camp in Afghanistan. He fits the profile of a terrorist in more ways than one.

Would-be shoe bomber Richard Reid, a British citizen, attended a mosque, dressed in Muslim clothing, spoke Arabic, and used various Muslim names.

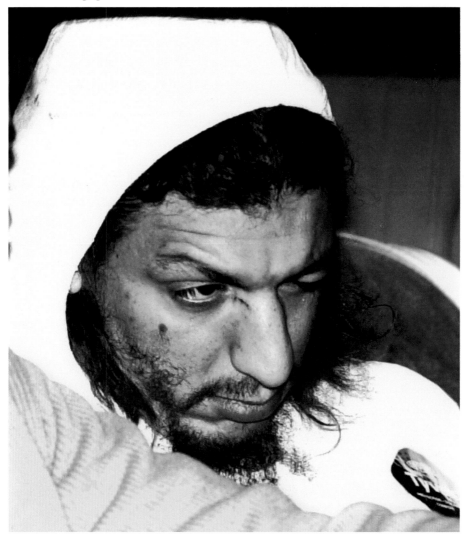

Besides, that there are exceptions to the rule doesn't mean there's no rule.

The fact that profiling won't identify *every* jihadist doesn't make it useless, or wrong. It will identify enough of them to help prevent bloodbaths that *will* occur if law enforcement officers and airport screeners *don't* cast an extra-watchful eye on youngish Muslims of North African, Middle Eastern or South East Asian descent.

Muslims Should Understand Why They Are Scrutinized

Argument Two: Focusing on Muslims alienates the very people—peaceful members of Muslim communities—whose tips authorities rely on to help them catch terrorists.

Muslims will have to face the music just like everyone else. Again, the radicals who would visit large-scale violence upon innocent civilians are not Italian septuagenarians or high-school-age Chilean exchange students. If I were a law-abiding Muslim in my prime, I believe I'd understand why screeners would want to take a closer look at me and my luggage, and why law enforcement officials might take an interest in my affiliations. It would all be burdensome and inconvenient, for sure—invasive, even. But it would only *strengthen* my desire to help root out potential mass murderers who, after all, *cause* all that scrutiny, and who abuse and insult my faith to justify their actions. I'd also understand—from taking an unflinching look at terrorism's bloody record—why police officers and intelligence operators would focus more on Muslim areas than on Hindu communities and Amish neighborhoods.

FAST FACT

A 2005 FOX News poll found that 42 percent of Americans approve of using racial profiling to catch suspected terrorists.

Profiling Techniques Should Be Combined

Argument Three: Ethnic profiling is unnecessary. Behavior profiling—looking for signs of unusual conduct, such as avoiding eye contact and sweating profusely—is both more palatable and more effective.

Why would it have to be a matter of either/or? Combining the two approaches is likely to be the most effective of all. No one is saying that people who don't fit the typical terrorist's profile never warrant a second look. Suspicious behavior should obviously be a red flag no matter who displays it—and doubly so when the person fits the ethnic and age profile. . . .

Nothing about ethnic profiling needs to signify a lack of respect, courtesy, or professionalism. People, no matter their color, creed, or nationality, will continue to be innocent until proof to the contrary is established. . . .

[But] it simply doesn't hold water to insist on subjecting Southern Baptists, Scottish pensioners and kindergartners from Paducah to the same scrutiny as young Muslim men, for fear of offending the latter.

Suspicion falls more easily on Muslims because Muslims have turned out to be responsible for one major terrorist act after another. No amount of pussyfooting or sugarcoating will change that fact. The sooner all sides face it honestly and squarely, the safer we all will be.

EVALUATING THE AUTHORS' ARGUMENTS:

Rogier van Bakel argues that law enforcement officials should not waste their time searching the general public for terrorists but should focus on people who fit a very specific set of characteristics. What main problem do you think the author of the following viewpoint, Daniel Moeckli, would have with this course of action?

Racial Profiling Violates Civil Liberties

Daniel Moeckli

> *"Ethnic profiling practices have proved largely unsuccesful. . . . Even worse, ethnic profiling may be counterproductive."*

In the following viewpoint Daniel Moeckli argues that racial profiling is not a legitimate way to catch terrorists. For one thing, Moeckli says, it does not work—terrorists are adapting beyond such profiles and increasingly feature women rather than men, and nationals rather than immigrants, in their plots. When police are looking for only a certain set of ethnic qualities, they are more likely to miss other people who are terrorists. Moeckli says in addition to being ineffective, racial profiling violates the civil liberties of countless numbers of people by making them targets of suspicion simply because of the way they look. He says a more serious way to catch terrorists is to focus on suspicious behavior rather than on race or ethnicity.

Moeckli is the author of *Human Rights and Non-discrimination in the "War on Terror."*

Daniel Moeckli, "The Impossibility of Terrorist Profiling," *OpenDemocracy.net*, December 9, 2008. Reproduced by permission. This article was originally published in the independent online magazine *www.opendemocracy.net*.

1. According to the author, how much more likely are Asian people to be stopped by police than white people in the United Kingdom? What about black people?
2. What do the words "over-inclusive" and "under-inclusive" mean in the context of the viewpoint?
3. Name at least three international human rights committees the author says reject the use of ethnicity as part of terrorist profiles.

A new report by MI5, the British domestic security service, challenges existing stereotypes about those involved in terrorism in the UK [United Kingdom]. The main findings of the classified "operational briefing note" have already been disclosed in the press. The report, which apparently is based on several hundred case studies, reveals that British-based terrorists fit "no single demographic profile." Most of them are male, but women also play an important role. The majority are British nationals, not illegal immigrants. There is a high proportion of conversion. Importantly, MI5 concludes that "assumptions cannot be made about suspects based on skin colour, ethnic heritage or nationality."

Yet exactly such assumptions have informed British anti-terrorism policing in recent years. Government officials and high-level police officers have made it clear that law enforcement efforts should focus on certain ethnic groups. The then Home Office Minister, Hazel Blears, implied that stop and searches under the Terrorism Act 2000 will "inevitably be disproportionately experienced by people in the Muslim community." Similarly, the Chief Constable of the British Transport Police has stated: "We should not waste time searching old white ladies. . . . It is going to be young men, not exclusively, but it may be disproportionate when it comes to ethnic groups."

Guilt by Pigmentation

Accordingly, the overall rise in anti-terrorism stop and searches (from 8,550 in 2001/02 to 37,197 in 2006/07) has mainly affected ethnic minorities. In the first two months after the London bombings of July 2005, for instance, the number of Asian and black people stopped

Critics of racial profiling point to a report by MI5, Britain's domestic security service, that found British-based terrorists fit no single demographic profile, making the procedure useless.

in the London metropolitan area increased twelvefold; for white people the increase was fivefold. The latest UK-wide figures show that Asian people are now 4.1 times more likely, and black people 4.5 times more likely, to be stopped and searched under the Terrorism Act 2000 than white people.

Not only in the UK is "ethnic profiling" one of the central tools of law enforcement agencies in their fight against terrorism. A study of police stops and document checks on the Moscow metro system, which are often carried out in response to terrorist threats, found that persons of non-Slavic appearance are 21.8 times more likely to be stopped than Slavs. In the United States, the immigration authorities adopted a series of policies and practices designed to counter terrorism that single out immigrants who are citizens of, or were born in, countries that have predominantly Arab and/or Muslim populations. In Germany, the police forces tried to identify terrorist "sleepers" by searching several million personal data sets for people matching the following profile: male;

age 18–40; current or former student; Muslim denomination or link through birth or nationality to one of several specified countries with a predominantly Muslim population . . . (the German Federal Constitutional Court declared this data mining operation unconstitutional).

Terrorist Profiles Based on Race Are Useless

As the MI5 report highlights, these kinds of terrorist profiles are useless and, indeed, misleading. Profiles that are based on such characteristics as ethnic appearance or national origin are inaccurate and highly over-inclusive, covering countless persons who are in no way linked to terrorism. At the same time, the stereotypical image of the male "Arab," "Middle Eastern" or "Asian" terrorist is also under-inclusive: it does not cover women or converts.

It is therefore not surprising that ethnic profiling practices have proved largely unsuccessful. In 2003/04, for example, 8,120 pedestrians were stopped in the UK under the Terrorism Act. Yet these stops led to only five arrests in connection with terrorism—a "success rate" of 0.06 percent. In-

> **FAST FACT**
>
> According to a 2009 report by the Open Society Institute, the personal data of 8.3 million people were searched in a massive German data-mining exercise that targeted—among other characteristics—people who were Muslim, and that did not identify a single terrorist.

cidentally, all of those arrested were white. In the United States, the strategy of mainly targeting immigrants of Middle Eastern descent has not produced any significant results in the form of arrests or investigative leads. And the German data mining programme did not result in a single criminal charge for terrorism-related offences.

An Ineffective Tool

Even worse, ethnic profiling may be counter-productive. Profiles based on ethnicity can shift the attention of police officers away from more pertinent indicators such as behavioural patterns or psychological characteristics. In addition, ethnic profiling contributes to the stigmatisation and alienation of the targeted minority groups. This stigmatisation,

Racial Profiling Is Not an Appropriate Law Enforcement Technique

A slim majority of Americans say they disapprove of using racial profiling to catch suspected terrorists.

"In general, do you approve or disapprove of using racial or ethnic profiling in the fight against terrorism?"

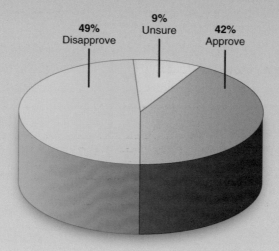

49%
Disapprove

9%
Unsure

42%
Approve

Taken from: Fox News/Opinion Dynamics poll, July 26–27, 2005.

in turn, may increase the distrust of the police and thus have significant negative implications for law-enforcement efforts.

Apart from these serious doubts about its suitability as a counter-terrorism tool, ethnic profiling also raises concerns with regard to its conformity with human rights standards, in particular the prohibition of discrimination. In a case before the House of Lords concerning the stop and search powers under the Terrorism Act 2000, some of their Lordships found that it is permissible for the police to rely on a person's Asian appearance as long as ethnicity is used in combination with further factors. Yet this test is not only unclear (Would it be enough for the police to simply add one additional factor, for example gender, to the profile? Or does it depend on the importance attached to the different factors?), but also runs counter to pronouncements of international human rights bodies.

Numerous Bodies Reject Racial Profiling

The UN [United Nations] Committee on the Elimination of Racial Discrimination, the UN Special Rapporteur on terrorism and human rights, the European Commission against Racism and Intolerance and the EU [European Union] Network of Independent Experts in Fundamental Rights have all warned against the use of ethnicity as part of terrorist profiles. As the UN Special Rapporteur has pointed out, the differential treatment that ethnic profiling involves could only be compatible with the prohibition of discrimination if it was supported by objective and reasonable grounds. But, he concluded, given its ineffectiveness and its adverse effects, ethnic profiling regularly fails to meet this requirement and is therefore discriminatory.

These human rights bodies have called for a number of concrete steps to prevent counter-terrorism practices based on ethnic profiling. For example, they have urged states to use random security checks as an alternative to profiling, establish systems of transparent and independent oversight of law enforcement agencies and implement training programmes for law enforcement agents. Perhaps the most effective training for law enforcement agents, but also for politicians, would be to require them to read the MI5 report.

EVALUATING THE AUTHORS' ARGUMENTS:

Daniel Moeckli argues that it is easy for terrorists to get around racial profiling by incorporating women, nationals, or converts into their terrorist plots. How do you think Rogier van Bakel, author of the previous viewpoint, would refute this argument? With whom do you ultimately agree?

Chapter 3

Should Limits Ever Be Placed on Free Speech?

Thousands of Muslims protest in the streets of Karachi, Pakistan, after Danish newspapers printed cartoons depicting the Prophet Muhammad.

Viewpoint 1

Offensive Speech Should Not Be Limited

David Harsanyi

"If we're not careful, the war against offensive speech could morph into a war against free speech."

Offensive speech should always be protected, argues David Harsanyi in the following viewpoint. Harsanyi discusses cases in which unpopular or offensive speech has been protested or even banned. In his opinion, the public should be able to cope with speech that is offensive or provocative, and he says this is one way in which open, democratic societies explore different and controversial ideas. Furthermore, once offensive or unpopular speech becomes subject to bans, Harsanyi worries that other forms of speech—such as political dissent or government criticism—will also be subject to censorship. For this reason, he thinks that all speech —even offensive or unpopular speech— deserves to be protected.

Harsanyi is a columnist at the *Denver Post* and the author of the book *Nanny State*.

David Harsanyi, "The Right Not to Be Offended?" *Denver Post*, February 25, 2009, Opinion. Copyright © 2009 by *Denver Post*. Distributed by Creators Syndicate, Inc. Reproduced by permission of Creators Syndicate, Inc.

I t's a discredit to our national confidence that each time some impolite thought—perceived or otherwise—is uttered, sketched, or typed, a faction of professionally offended Americans engages in a collective hypersensitivity meltdown.

We Are Too Sensitive About Speech

It has been a long-standing custom for opponents to shut down debate by tagging adversaries with some dreadful labels. No one wants to be called a racist, a Commie, or a neocon. It's gotten to the point that the gatekeepers of the news walk so tepidly on the path of least resistance a journalist can't even get a dirty joke in the newspaper.

Attorney General Eric Holder recently claimed that we, as a nation, have been cowards on the topic of race. And maybe he's right. Some Americans are cowards. Other Americans—the ones in the media—worry that [African American activist] Al Sharpton might show up in their doorways and shake down their kids for allowance money.

Hysteria over a Cartoon

Sean Delonas, cartooning at the *New York Post*, recently learned what happens when you inadvertently offend. He equated congressional authors of the so-called stimulus bill with that crazy rampaging chimpanzee[1] (admittedly an unpardonable insult to our simian cousins). But some readers saw Barack Obama. So the situation has erupted into a massively stupid kerfuffle.

Now, I don't doubt that many readers of this admittedly unfortunate cartoon legitimately were offended. So let's, for the sake of argument, concede that the cartoonist is a raging racist. What now?

1. In February 2009 a woman was attacked by a friend's pet chimpanzee in Connecticut and sustained severe injuries.

In protests this week, students at a New York college urged boycotts, began burning newspapers—a hop, skip, and jump from burning books!—and demanded that anyone involved with the cartoon be fired. Fair enough.

But now the Rev. Al has ordered a meeting with the Federal Communications Commission [FCC] so he—a man who has set off more chaos, loathing, and racism in New York than any cartoonist—can discuss the ownership of the *Post*. The FCC, according to Sharpton, has acquiesced to meet in Washington.

As an antiquated government entity, the FCC controls the public airwaves and ownership of media companies. What if it meets with Sharpton and then moves against the *New York Post*'s owner?

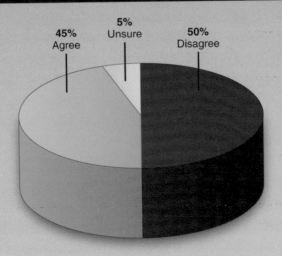

More Americans Think Even Offensive Speech Should Be Protected

A 2007 Pew Research Center poll found that a slim majority of Americans think that even terrorist speech should be protected by the First Amendment. A full half of the American public disagreed with the suggestion that free speech should not apply to groups sympathetic to terrorists.

"Do you agree or disagree that freedom of speech should *not* be extended to groups that are sympathetic to terrorists?"

45%
Agree

5%
Unsure

50%
Disagree

Taken from: Pew Research Center for the People & the Press survey conducted by Princeton Survey Research Associates International, December 12, 2006–January 9, 2007.

Stifling Offensive Speech Is Dangerous

We largely have avoided the corrosive trend of chilling free speech—though discussions about the "Fairness Doctrine" (and its derivatives), which allows government to dictate what opinions Americans should hear on the public airwaves, remains a hobbyhorse for some [politically liberal] lefties.

A media outlet, of course, is under no obligation to print something that gratuitously offends readers, and it would be counterproductive for it to do so. But umbrage often is taken regardless. Should an angry conservative leader have met with the FCC to discuss the future of the *Washington Post*'s ownership when one of the paper's cartoonists depicted an American solider as a suicide bomber a few years ago? Imagine the outrage such a move would have caused.

Because Dutch politician Geert Wilders' film Fitna *was found to encourage violence and extremism, he was refused entry into the United Kingdom. The nation has established a policy designed to block the spread of hatred and violence.*

Any Suppression of Speech Is Worrisome

Recently, Geert Wilders—a Dutch politician who produced the film "Fitna," which asserts that Islam is a threat to enlightened Western values—was refused entry into the United Kingdom because of that nation's policy to "stop those who want to spread extremism, hatred and violent messages."

The British proved Wilders' point about Islam's influence by suppressing free expression. The case of Wilders, who is in the U.S. right now, offers a cautionary lesson.

Feel free to be indignant and hurt. Feel free to boycott and to cast nasty aspersions on the decency of those who offend you. But let's keep government out of it. If we're not careful, the war against offensive speech could morph into a war against free speech.

EVALUATING THE AUTHOR'S ARGUMENTS:

David Harsanyi thinks the situation that erupted over a potentially racist *New York Post* cartoon was at best stupid and at worst a threat to free speech. What do you think? Based on his description of the cartoon, what do you think an appropriate course of action would have been? Should the people involved with the cartoon have been fired? Should the *Post*'s owners be held accountable? Or did everyone make too much of the incident?

Free Speech Should Sometimes Be Limited

Randal Marlin

"Freedom of expression is never an absolute."

In the following viewpoint Randal Marlin argues that free speech has and should have several limits. In fact, Marlin says free speech is limited all the time—this is essentially the point of copyright laws, laws against misleading advertising, and speaking contemptibly in court. He discusses a case in Canada in which anti-Israeli posters were banned by two universities. Marlin says that some people interpreted the posters as political statements, and thus thought banning them was a violation of free speech. But Marlin thinks the posters demonized Israelis to such an unfair degree that censoring the posters was the right thing to do because they added nothing constructive to any conversation about the Israeli-Palestinian conflict. He concludes that free speech is not supposed to be an absolute free-for-all—if the speech is not constructive or demonizes groups of people, it should be subject to censorship.

Marlin is a professor of philosophy at Carleton University in Ottawa, Ontario, Canada, and is also the author of *Propaganda and the Ethics of Persuasion* (2002, Broadview Press).

AS YOU READ, CONSIDER THE FOLLOWING QUESTIONS
1. What are some of the limits to free expression that Marlin describes as commonplace in society?
2. What is the content of a "Toy Soldier" advertisement, as discussed by Marlin?
3. What policy does Marlin think the Israeli helicopter poster violated?

Recent controversies over proposed atheist messages on buses and anti-Israeli posters at Carleton and Ottawa universities serve as a reminder that free speech issues are often complex. Freedom of expression is never an absolute, as the continued, justifiable existence of libel laws makes plain. In Ireland the right to one's good name is constitutionally entrenched on a par with free speech.

There Are Many Acceptable Limits to Free Speech
Copyright, contempt of court, contractual agreements to secrecy, misleading advertising, incitement, hate propaganda—the list of limitations to freedom of expression goes on. In each area cases can be found where undue weight is given to one side or the other of the balance.

A surprisingly long list of values can conflict with free expression. Clutter from posters on telephone poles may annoy some while others rejoice at the opportunity for hard up artists to express themselves and advertise events. Noise pollution from bullhorns may also create resentment. In both cases, one can envisage a municipal bylaw of limited scope being justifiable because it is aimed at restricting the form of a message rather than content.

Policy-making may be involved. Some years ago the Toronto Transit Commission turned down a "Toy Soldier" advertisement conveying the message that the soldier would have so many fewer children to play with because of so many abortions. Despite initial approval,

Just How Free Is America's Press?

Although the United States is known for its freedom of expression, it only ranks number 21 on a list of countries with free presses compiled by the organization Freedom House. It lost points for having excessively partisan media, threats of violence against journalists, and for government leakage of sources.

Rank 2008	Country
1	Finland
	Iceland
3	Denmark
	Norway
5	Belgium
	Sweden
7	Luxembourg
8	Andorra
	Netherlands
	New Zealand
	Switzerland
12	Liechtenstein
	Palau
14	Ireland
	Jamaica
16	Estonia
	Germany
	Monaco
	Portugal
	St. Lucia
21	Marshall Islands
	San Marino
	St. Vincent and Grenadines
	United States
25	Canada
	Czech Republic
	Lithuania
	United Kingdom
29	Barbados
	Costa Rica
	St. Kitts and Nevis

Taken from: Freedom House, "Freedom of the Press 2008: Table of Global Press Freedom Rankings," 2009.

the advertisement was withdrawn following a strong editorial in the *Toronto Star* about how this would offend many women.

Many Things to Consider

In a recent excellent *Citizen* article by Don Butler, the point was made by Alan Borovoy, general counsel of the Canadian Civil Liberties Association, that fear of giving offence had led to too much restriction on freedom of expression, such as the suppression of the Gaza poster announcing anti-Israeli Apartheid week. Those who agree with Mr. Borovoy on this point should ask whether giving the principle of free speech precedence over people taking offence should not also involve them in rejecting the Toronto Transit Commission's decision.

My own view is that the issue is not clear-cut. A transit authority has to decide what its policy will be with regard to advertising, given that people may have reason to take offence at what is displayed. The policy would have to concern itself with reasonable taking of offence, and not just any subjective dislike. It might decide to accept no advocacy advertising, or only such advertising deemed to be inoffensive and in good taste. Displays of war victims with missing body parts might be seen to be too upsetting. Here a committee might be struck to judge such matters.

> **FAST FACT**
>
> A study by the John S. and James L. Knight Foundation found that only half of the students surveyed feel that newspapers should be allowed to publish stories without the government's approval.

As long as a transit authority decides it will accept controversial advocacy advertising, there seems little reason to reject an advertisement on behalf of the atheist cause. But the same policy should then permit religious advocacy as well. The end result may be to stimulate debate, a good thing, or it might degenerate into rousing old feelings of enmity, a bad thing.

Some Messages Go Too Far

In the case of Carleton and Ottawa universities, the prohibited poster was susceptible to different interpretations. I saw it as portraying an

Two Canadian Universities, Ottowa and Carleton, banned the display of anti-Israel posters. The author contends that this action was not a violation of free speech because the posters unfairly demonized Israelis.

Israeli helicopter deliberately aiming a missile at a small solitary Gazan child carrying a teddy bear. To me, this said that the Israeli was deliberately targeting a small child, with no offensive weaponry anywhere nearby, thus portraying a special kind of cruelty, sadism and monstrosity that could hardly avoid creating hatred towards the perpetrator of this deed.

I happen to share the condemnation of the Israeli attack on Gaza as grossly disproportionate and unjustifiable. I can accept also that whether intentional or not, the killing of some 200–400 children (the highest estimate I've seen was 431), or anything near that, was unconscionable. But the poster took an extra step, portraying the mind of the Israeli operating the helicopter (whether directly or by remote) as gratuitously cruel and evil.

When Speech Discriminates, It Can Be Limited

It is true that cartoons get their message across through exaggeration. One should not, one is told, interpret with a high degree of specificity. Innocent children were killed, and according to one account a few older children were indeed targeted while playing soccer. Therefore banning the poster was wrong.

But Carleton University has a policy dealing with anti-racism, where "race" is stipulated to mean "race, ancestry, place or origin, colour, ethnic origin, or citizenship." The policy involves the prohibition of discrimination and harassment including conduct on the basis of race (as defined) that is "abusive, demeaning or threatening including . . . display of derogatory or belittling pictures and graffiti."

My own feeling is that the poster could easily be found in violation of that policy, by its imputing gratuitous cruelty to the helicopter controller. This was identified with the State of Israel and could easily tap into long-standing anti-Semitic false tales of child-killing. Not everyone will see this, but I see it as one of several possible reasonable interpretations of the poster's impact. Carleton University is committed in its policy to addressing practices that "while not intentionally discriminatory, have a discriminatory effect."

The Right Decision

Censorship in the form of "prior restraint," is especially abhorrent because typically the public has no way of knowing what is being censored, and the censors' decision escapes public scrutiny. But such was not the case here. The question was whether approval of wide display of the poster would violate university policy. Banning it would take away a (minimal) seal of approval, without stopping people seeing it as they could always go on the Internet and search for "Israel Anti-Apartheid Week, Gaza poster."

Given these overall circumstances, I see the university decision as defensible.

EVALUATING THE AUTHORS' ARGUMENTS:

Randal Marlin focuses his argument on a poster that features an Israeli helicopter pilot shooting a missile at a Palestinian child. What do you think David Harsanyi, author of the previous viewpoint, would think of this poster? What would he say about the university's decision to ban it? After summarizing Harsanyi's thoughts, state your own. With which author do you agree on whether free speech should have limits?

The Speech of Students Should Be Limited

Selwyn Duke

"The truth is that students do not have freedom of speech in school. Why, we can spew profanity at others on the street . . . but a student may be punished if he directs [the] same at a teacher."

Students are not protected by the First Amendment's right to free speech, argues Selwyn Duke in the following viewpoint. He discusses a recent Supreme Court case that ruled as much, and explains why. Students are minors, he reminds readers, and as such they are not granted a full set of rights. They cannot buy alcohol, drive, vote, get married, or join the military. It makes sense to Duke that free speech would be among the rights that students do not have access to while still in school. Furthermore, Duke thinks pretending that students should be able to say whatever they like in school is wrong. Just as students are not allowed to curse at teachers, so too should they be unable to make inflammatory, racist, or illegal statements. Duke concludes that schools are one of many public institutions at which free speech is not an acceptable or applicable freedom.

Selwyn Duke, "Free Speech from the Mouths of Babes?" *American Thinker*, June 28, 2008. Reproduced by permission of the author.

Duke's articles have appeared in *American Thinker*, in which this viewpoint was originally published.

AS YOU READ, CONSIDER THE FOLLOWING QUESTIONS:
1. What was Supreme Court Justice Clarence Thomas's conclusion in the case *Morse et al. v. Frederick*?
2. What right does Duke say everyone can agree should not be extended to minors?
3. What other public institutions place limits on free speech, according to Duke?

On Monday [June 25, 2007] the Supreme court handed down three free speech rulings that find favor with conservatives. One of them is *Morse et al. v. Frederick*, a case involving the free speech rights of students. At issue is a five-year-old incident wherein a Juneau-Douglas [Alaska] High School senior named Joe Frederick raised a 14-foot banner stating "Bong Hits 4 Jesus" and was subsequently suspended for "drug speech" by then school principal Deborah Morse. Writing for the majority in a five to four decision in favor of the school, Chief Justice John Roberts reasoned that the First Amendment should not be applied in this case because the student was encouraging drug use. . . .

Students Should Shed Their Rights at the "Schoolhouse Gate"

The real issue here extends far beyond this one case and harks back to a precedent set in 1969 in the *Tinker v. Des Moines* ruling, which divined from the Constitution a right to free speech in schools. Upon issuance of that decision the court stated,

> It can hardly be argued that either students or teachers shed their constitutional rights to freedom of speech or expression at the schoolhouse gate.

Really? What can hardly be argued is that the donning of a black robe confers intelligence, wisdom or even much useful knowledge upon the wearer.

In writing for the majority opinion in Morse et al. v. Frederick, *Supreme Court Justice Clarence Thomas (pictured) declared that the First Amendment does not encompass a student's right to speak in public schools.*

The truth here can be found in one of the few bright spots in [the *Morse et al. v. Frederick*] case. Writing in his concurrence, Justice Clarence Thomas drove to the heart of the matter in saying,

> . . . it cannot seriously be suggested that the First Amendment "Freedom of speech" encompasses a student's right to speak in public schools.

Minors Do Not Enjoy Full Rights

Leftists can argue till they're blue in the face, but the truth is that students *do not* have freedom of speech in school. Why, we can spew profanity at

They suspended you for your "Bong Hits 4 Jesus" stunt?!?

It's great! This is how talentless people become famous.

PRINCIPAL'S OFFICE

"They Suspended You for Your 'Bong Hits 4 Jesus' Stunt?!" cartoon by Stu's Views, case of *Morse v. Frederick*. Reprinted with permission of Stu's Views. Copyright © Stu Rees, www.Stus.com.

others on the street—in fact, some people where I grew up in NYC consider it a pastime—but a student may be punished if he directs same at a teacher or peer. I also have to wonder if the left's highly principled stand in defense of free speech would be maintained in the face of a student given to Nazi and white supremacist rhetoric.

The fact is that we don't ascribe to minors an adult set of rights. Minors may not buy alcohol or cigarettes, drive before a certain age, join the military, get married or enter into other kinds of legal contracts. Most tellingly, while enshrined in the Constitution is, "A well regulated militia being necessary to the security of a free State, the right of the People to keep and bear arms shall not be infringed," there isn't much clamor to extend this right to minors.

Free Speech Is a Facade

In ignoring this, the more conservative members of the court are guilty of the same reasoning, if not the same sanctimony, as the left. Virtually no one supports granting "free speech" to students; that is, free speech properly understood. As I've said before, freedom of speech is but a facade unless the guarantee protects even the most odious, most offensive, most unpopular speech of all. Popular sentiments require no legal protection, as their popularity is protection enough. Thus, to draw the distinctions we already have—oh, such as proscribing "hate speech" on school grounds (remember, we may spew whatever hatred we wish, even the faux variety the thought police hate so much)—is to tacitly acknowledge that there is *no free speech* in that arena. (Note: This isn't a violation of the Constitution because the original intent of its framers is what rightly governs the document's application, and it's unreasonable to believe these 18th century men would have granted children the right to be sassy brats.)

Many Institutions Do Not Allow Free Speech

Schools also are not alone as governmental institutions that prohibit free speech. Most obviously, military personnel are quite limited in the use of the tongue, and police departments come to mind as well. In fact, with sexual harassment and hate speech codes becoming the stuff of bureaucratic rubric, it may be hard to find an American governmental entity that affords its workers that most important American freedom. And while I definitely dislike the way this principle of censorship is applied by our Orwellian[1] puppeteers, the principle itself is sound. Only the most delusional egalitarian fails to understand that for a society to function properly, just hierarchies must be operative and respected. . . .

FAST FACT

A Gallup Youth Survey of thirteen- to seventeen-year-old students revealed that 75 percent believe it is acceptable for public schools to restrict bad language in writing assignments.

---

1. *Orwellian* refers to British novelist George Orwell's *1984*, a work about repressive government.

What this boils down to is that, after all the intellectual contortions and philoso-babble, the court is saying something very simple: Students shouldn't be allowed to say certain things.

EVALUATING THE AUTHOR'S ARGUMENTS:

To make his argument, Selwyn Duke points out all the rights and freedoms that are not afforded to students under certain ages. What are these rights and freedoms? Do you think that free speech belongs in this category? Why or why not?

The Speech of Students Should Not Be Limited

Donal Brown

"Even when students misstep, a freer atmosphere enables students to learn the lessons of democracy."

In the following viewpoint Donal Brown argues against limiting the speech of students. He says that students deserve to be treated like adults so they can become familiar and comfortable with the complexities and challenges of issues like democracy and free speech. If their speech is censored, they have no opportunity to learn; but if their speech is discussed in an open environment, they can learn what sentiments are appropriate and fair to express, and why. Far more dangerous than granting students free speech, says Brown, is granting principals the ability to censor them. In this environment, students cannot learn about the importance of a free press or consider opinions different from their own. For all of these reasons, Brown disagrees with court decisions that take speech rights away from students and give censorship abilities to school administrators.

Brown is a reporter for New America Media, a national collaboration and advocate of two thousand ethnic news organizations.

AS YOU READ, CONSIDER THE FOLLOWING QUESTIONS:
1. Who is Deborah Morse, and how does she factor into the author's argument?
2. What did the Supreme Court find in the case of *Hazelwood v. Kuhlmeier*, as reported by Brown?
3. What does censorship force student journalists to report on? Why does Brown think this is a problem?

Supreme Court Justice Stephen Breyer should spend some time in a public school. That might equip him to make a more intelligent decision in the case argued before the court this week [in March 2007], pitting a principal against a student suspended for unveiling a 14-foot banner reading "Bong Hists 4 Jesus" as the 2002 Olympic torch was carried through the streets of Juneau, Alaska.

In trying to sum up the choice for the Supreme Court, Breyer said that if the court rules for the student, there would be students across the country testing authority in disruptive ways and if it rules for the principal, school administrators could use the decision to curtail free speech.

A Lost Opportunity to Educate

The student, Joseph Frederick, claimed the banner was only intended to put him on TV. That it did. But foolish, distasteful acts have a way of becoming a focus of landmark cases and such is the case with *Morse v. Frederick*. The principal, Deborah Morse, was incensed by the outrageous nature of Frederick's message and ultimately suspended him for 10 days when he wouldn't finger his accomplices.

Some commentators have criticized Morse for turning Frederick into a poster boy for freedom of speech when he was only interested in bringing attention to himself. That aside, the principal lost an opportunity to educate Frederick and his peers in the importance of free speech and, along with it, responsibilities in using restraint and good taste in a public forum.

In Juneau, Alaska, high school principal Deborah Morse became one of the parties in a First Amendment court case when she suspended student Joseph Frederick.

How Else Will Students Learn to Be Adult Citizens?
It is too often the tendency of principals to think first of mollifying the adult community and giving little thought to the opportunity to educate students. Ensuing court cases can provide education, but it is also important to devote class time to discuss vital issues at the time they arise. In too many instances, the punishment becomes the focus rather than principles and values.

Once, at the high school where I taught journalism, a male student on the school's Model United Nations team wore a dress to an awards ceremony. He was punished by the administration, but reporters with the student newspaper that I advised could not get the vice principal to explain why he thought it was wrong to wear the dress. How can students learn to be functioning adults unless adults explain their values and expectations?

Censorship Is More Dangerous Than Free Speech

From my 35 years in California's public schools and teaching about free speech and free press, it is my opinion that there is little chance of students unleashing a barrage of senseless free speech pranks. But there is a real danger of principals using the case to curtail student expression.

In the first place, it is unlikely that students will have heard of the case even after the Supreme Court decides it. Ask students if they know about *Tinker v. Des Moines*, the famous case decided in 1969 that held that students did not shed their free speech rights when they walked into the school, and I'll bet that fewer than one in a thousand have even heard of the case, much less know any of its salient details.

Nor is it a given that outside of Frederick's peer group, students thought it was cool to unfurl the banner, "Bong Hits 4 Jesus." After a jury acquitted the police officers in the Rodney King beating, a student led a march during school hours for ten miles to the Golden Gate Bridge. On the way she ignored the entreaties of a vice principal to make the march safer for students. Even though most of the student body did not approve of the verdict, they sided with the administration and harshly criticized the girl for what they viewed as self-aggrandizing actions. The local press could not understand why so many students sided with adult authority.

While it is not a given that students will act in immature ways more than is their natural bent, it's loading a cannon to give administrators more discretion in shutting down free expression. You can bet they will know of *Morse v. Frederick*.

Freedom Is Always Better

The 1988 Supreme Court case *Hazelwood v. Kuhlmeier* held that principals could act as editors to alter "the style and content of student"

Supreme Court Rulings on Students and Free Speech

Since 1969, the Supreme Court has handed down several decisions that have affected the speech rights of students.

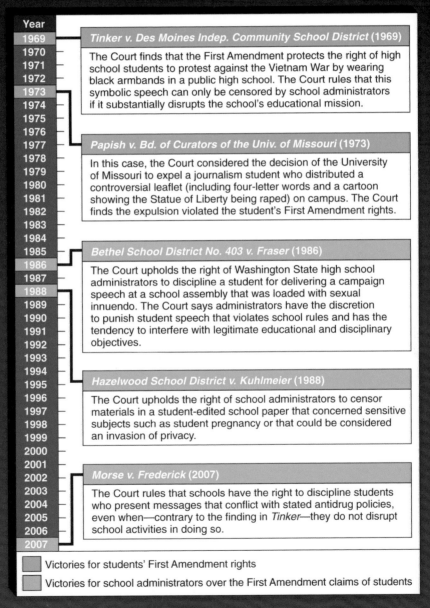

Year	
1969	**Tinker v. Des Moines Indep. Community School District (1969)**
1970	The Court finds that the First Amendment protects the right of high
1971	school students to protest against the Vietnam War by wearing
1972	black armbands in a public high school. The Court rules that this
1973	symbolic speech can only be censored by school administrators
1974	if it substantially disrupts the school's educational mission.
1975	
1976	
1977	**Papish v. Bd. of Curators of the Univ. of Missouri (1973)**
1978	In this case, the Court considered the decision of the University
1979	of Missouri to expel a journalism student who distributed a
1980	controversial leaflet (including four-letter words and a cartoon
1981	showing the Statue of Liberty being raped) on campus. The Court
1982	finds the expulsion violated the student's First Amendment rights.
1983	
1984	
1985	**Bethel School District No. 403 v. Fraser (1986)**
1986	The Court upholds the right of Washington State high school
1987	administrators to discipline a student for delivering a campaign
1988	speech at a school assembly that was loaded with sexual
1989	innuendo. The Court says administrators have the discretion
1990	to punish student speech that violates school rules and has the
1991	tendency to interfere with legitimate educational and disciplinary
1992	objectives.
1993	
1994	
1995	**Hazelwood School District v. Kuhlmeier (1988)**
1996	The Court upholds the right of school administrators to censor
1997	materials in a student-edited school paper that concerned sensitive
1998	subjects such as student pregnancy or that could be considered
1999	an invasion of privacy.
2000	
2001	
2002	**Morse v. Frederick (2007)**
2003	The Court rules that schools have the right to discipline students
2004	who present messages that conflict with stated antidrug policies,
2005	even when—contrary to the finding in *Tinker*—they do not disrupt
2006	school activities in doing so.
2007	

■ Victories for students' First Amendment rights
■ Victories for school administrators over the First Amendment claims of students

Taken from: Doug Linder, "Exploring Constitutional Law," University of Missouri–Kansas City School of Law, 2009.

speech so long as their intent was to serve legitimate educational goals. This was a blow to scholastic free press as principals became censors. Advisers whose jobs are frequently on the line for not censoring students become even more reluctant to allow students to investigate or criticize the principal.

Thus constrained, students do not learn the power of the free press and the responsibilities that go along with that freedom. And limited to reporting on bake sales and pep rallies, student reporters can't learn sophisticated lessons on fairness and accuracy.

I implore Justice Breyer and the eight other justices to fashion a decision that tips the balance in favor of free student expression. Even when students misstep, a freer atmosphere enables students to learn the lessons of democracy.

EVALUATING THE AUTHORS' ARGUMENTS:

Donal Brown and Selwyn Duke, author of the previous viewpoint, disagree on whether student speech should be limited. After considering both of their arguments, think of one example of controversial speech you might see at your school that you think should be tolerated, and one example that you think should be censored. Ultimately, what limits do you think should be placed on student speech?

Parts of the Internet Should Be Censored

Peter Grad

> "The umbrella of free speech was never intended to protect utterly offensive speech or comments that incite imminent harm, including murder."

In the following viewpoint Peter Grad argues that not everything online deserves to be protected. He focuses on videos uploaded to YouTube by terrorists, arguing that these do not deserve to be protected by the First Amendment. Some of the videos show the violent murder of innocent people; others are intended to encourage people to attack Americans, even children. Grad says such material does not contribute to a healthy debate or meaningfully impact society. He says the Internet should not be a platform for those who want to hurt Americans, and the right to free speech—one of the nation's most cherished values—should not be extended to the people who want to destroy the United States. For all of these reasons, Grad says that video-hosting sites should take down terrorist videos and not worry they are impinging on a terrorist's "right" to free speech.

Peter Grad, "Terrorists' Videos Don't Belong on YouTube," *Record* (Bergen County, NJ), May 31, 2008, p. F8, Better Living. Copyright © 2008 North Jersey Media Group, Inc. Reproduced by permission.

Grad writes a column called The PC Guy that is published in the *Bergen Record*, a New Jersey newspaper.

AS YOU READ, CONSIDER THE FOLLOWING QUESTIONS:
1. What did Senator Joseph Lieberman ask Google to do, according to Grad?
2. How does Grad describe the groups al-Qaeda and Ansar al-Islam?
3. In what ways does the author say YouTube is confused?

I've not been a big fan of Sen. Joseph Lieberman[1] since I voted for [Al] Gore and him in 2000, his gushing support for the president's course in Iraq a key, though not the sole, factor. But I think the senator is getting a bad rap on a recent dust-up concerning the Internet and the issue of free speech.

A Reasonable Request

Lieberman recently wrote to Google, which owns the popular video-sharing site YouTube, asking that it remove videos sponsored by terrorist organizations. His request seemed reasonable enough. "A great majority of these videos document horrific attacks on American soldiers in Iraq or Afghanistan," the senator said. Others detail weapons-training procedures to be used against enemies of the radical groups.

But he has drawn criticism in some quarters, including the *New York Times*, which slammed Lieberman in an editorial last week [May 2008]. It declared Lieberman a "censor" who is attempting to "demonize" the Internet, and found it "profoundly disturbing" that he would "consider telling a media company to shut down constitutionally protected speech."

We Cannot Condone Violent, Destructive Speech

The *Times'* confusion over censorship aside, Lieberman merely asked Google to observe its own guidelines against offensive materials; there were no threats or orders. The newspaper's notion of propriety in this case is troubling.

1. The senator ran for vice president in the 2000 presidential election.

Senator Joseph Lieberman (pictured) has called for terrorist-sponsored videos to be removed from the Internet, arguing that the videos have no redeeming value and should not be protected by the First Amendment.

Lieberman pointed to the appearance of dozens of videos housed on YouTube that are sponsored by terrorist organizations such as al-Qaida and Ansar al-Islam. These are not neighborhood benevolent associations or book discussion clubs. These organizations engage in violent, random destruction aimed at largely innocent victims. They recruit children to wear explosives and blow up themselves and others of the "wrong" religion or political persuasion. They have instigated massacres, and Ansar al-Islam has been tied to the beheading of 53 villagers.

Terrorists Do Not Contribute Meaningfully to Society

The *Times* and YouTube would have us believe that these videos are merely part of a community debate.

Too often, well-intentioned folks reflexively reach for the First Amendment when talk about the boundaries of speech is raised. It sounds nice to utter the words free speech and embrace the wonderful notion that however extreme the sentiments, the marketplace of ideas will nourish the sound ones and dispense with the poor ones. Such absolutists say, as the *Times* did, that "if we give up our fundamental rights [of unfettered speech], the terrorists win."

But the umbrella of free speech was never intended to protect utterly offensive speech or comments that incite imminent harm, including murder or mass destruction.

The First Amendment Is Not a Free-for-All

And despite our open embrace of robust discussion and minimal intrusion on the parameters of open debate, there has never been sanctuary within the First Amendment for the expression of certain vile beliefs: Strident advocacy of child molestation or rape is not protected speech. The First Amendment does not protect words or actions of Nazis or the Ku Klux Klan or anyone explicitly advocating harm to an individual, especially on the basis of race or religion. It gives no safe harbor to those who would reveal secret U.S. Army plans in the midst of battle. It does not shield an elementary school teacher who utters obscenities in a classroom. And an entire body of law has grown around the notion of libel, the irresponsible utterances of untrue or hurtful comments about others, which lies outside the boundary of protected speech.

> **FAST FACT**
>
> According to counter-terrorism expert Evan Kohlmann, 90 percent of terrorist activity on the Internet takes place using social networking tools such as independent bulletin boards, Paltalk, or Yahoo! eGroups.

Countries like Iran and China are famous for censoring the Internet. But a growing number of countries—many of which are democracies—are taking actions to censor their citizens' access to the Internet.

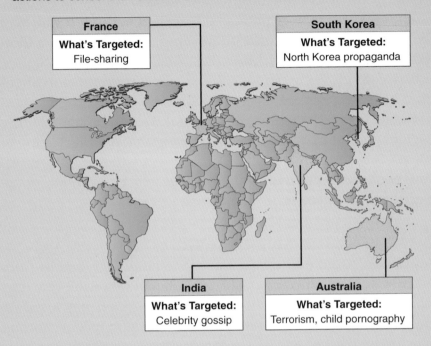

France		South Korea	
What's Targeted: File-sharing		**What's Targeted:** North Korea propaganda	

India		Australia	
What's Targeted: Celebrity gossip		**What's Targeted:** Terrorism, child pornography	

Taken from: Joshua Keating, "The List: Look Who's Censoring the Internet Now," *Foreign Policy*, March 2009.

Not Everything Online Contributes to Healthy Debate

Here is what YouTube said in response to Lieberman's letter:

> We believe that YouTube is a richer and more relevant platform for users precisely because it hosts a diverse range of views, and rather than stifle debate, we allow our users to view all acceptable content and make up their own minds. . . . Users are always free to express their disagreement . . . by leaving comments or their own response video. That debate is healthy.

Really? Would footage praising the slitting of the throat of American Daniel Pearl by terrorists be part of that "healthy" debate? Are propaganda films recruiting pre-teens to kill foreigners a "healthy" component on the debate on the Mideast? Are brutal acts of violence and degradation of women in music videos part of that "healthy" debate?

As blogger Mark Hopkins noted in a recent post, YouTube seems confused. The site, in fact, does observe some standards of decency, but without any apparent consistency. For instance, it yanked a video by a woman who created a montage of victims of terrorist attacks in the wake of the Mohammed cartoon controversy a few years back. YouTube said her montage promoted hate speech. But it permitted a video depicting homeless men pummeling each other after a film-maker offered them sandwiches as pay.

It barred a video of a rap song with derogatory comments about women but gave a free pass to pornographic ads. It also barred a video of a woman breast-feeding a child and yanked footage captured by a witness to police brutality. If there is any logic to YouTube's sense of propriety, it escapes me.

YouTube's own policy stipulates it will not tolerate videos of "someone getting hurt, attacked or humiliated."

It Is OK to Censor Abhorrent Videos

We can adhere to our principles of free and robust debate, but the *Times* should not fear that terrorists would "win" should reasonable restraints on abhorrent videos be made. The terrorists, however, may win if we befoul our language by redefining healthy debate to include hosting video clips by religious fanatics embracing and encouraging mutilations, beheadings and assassinations of "infidels."

Lieberman is on target in his request for a consistent YouTube policy, and he should be praised for his efforts.

EVALUATING THE AUTHOR'S ARGUMENTS:

Peter Grad thinks videos of beheadings and murders do not qualify as constitutionally protected free speech. What do you think? Do such images have any merit that is worthy of being protected under the First Amendment? Why or why not?

No Part of the Internet Should Be Censored

Fred Reed

> *"Automated censorship invariably ends up blocking much that it shouldn't. The results have been consistently absurd."*

The Internet should not be censored, argues Fred Reed in the following viewpoint. He discusses how pornography is everywhere online, and agrees that parents are right to be concerned about what their children are viewing. But in Reed's opinion, censoring the Internet is not the answer. For one thing, Reed says, censored Internet searches tend to block a lot of useful and legitimate material. Second, he thinks it would be impossible to actually censor the Internet—it is too large and rapidly changing, and it would require a massive, expensive bureaucracy with thousands of censors. Finally, Reed thinks it is dangerous to start drawing lines around material that should and should not be subject to censorship. He says someone will inevitably want to stifle speech that is politically or socially important. Reed thinks that Internet content should be fully protected by the First Amendment, and he warns against tumbling down the slippery slope of Internet censorship.

Fred Reed, "Should Online Porn Be Barred?" *Washington Times*, January 5, 2008, p. C11. Copyright © 2008 *Washington Times*. Reproduced by permission.

Reed is a technology columnist for the *Washington Times*, in which this viewpoint was originally printed.

AS YOU READ, CONSIDER THE FOLLOWING QUESTIONS:
1. Why does Reed think NetNanny.com is not a reasonable solution to blocking inappropriate online content?
2. What effect does Reed think online pornography has on young kids?
3. Who does not really like free speech, according to Reed?

Recently, I found myself discussing with a female friend the advisability of censoring pornography on the Internet. The idea of censoring the Net comes up time and again. Her argument: Children should not be able to see grotesque porn.

Today, they sure can. Any form of porn you can possibly imagine is out there, and probably many that you can't. Mere sadomasochism seems almost tame.

Further, you can be sure that adolescents look at whatever interests them, whether for reasons of libido or just curiosity.

Automated Censorship Blocks Good Content, Too

One sees ads for software aimed at blocking "inappropriate content," as for example NetNanny.com. This may work for children of 9.

In the case of boys of 15, it doesn't even come close. They are tech-savvy, often more so than their parents. Workarounds are easy to find. There is always another computer without NetNanny.

Further, automated censorship invariably ends up blocking much that it shouldn't. The results have been consistently absurd.

Which means the odds are that your daughter of 15 has seen things that a hardened denizen of New York's underground wouldn't have seen in days before the Web.

It Is Impossible to Censor the Internet

The question is, what effect does the availability of this stuff have on our kids? Does it damage their psyches? Or does the young lady say,

The Internet Is Too Big to Censor

The Internet grows annually by about 50 percent, adding millions of users and sites and a vast amount of content each year. Some say that its incredible growth rate makes it impossible to censor.

2002   Number of Internet users

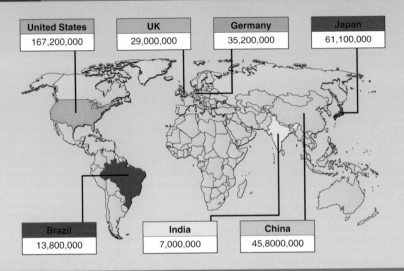

United States	UK	Germany	Japan
167,200,000	29,000,000	35,200,000	61,100,000

Brazil	India	China
13,800,000	7,000,000	45,8000,000

2008   Percentage of the country's population using the Internet

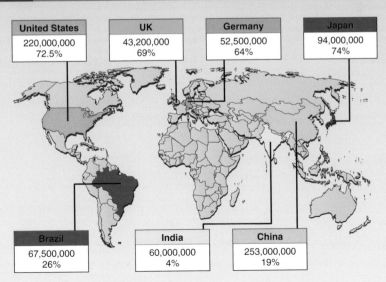

United States	UK	Germany	Japan
220,000,000	43,200,000	52,500,000	94,000,000
72.5%	69%	64%	74%

Brazil	India	China
67,500,000	60,000,000	253,000,000
26%	4%	19%

Taken from: *New Scientist*, "Exploring the Exploding Internet," 2009.

"Yuck! These people are sick," and become bored, and listen to her iPod instead? I note that it has already had whatever effect it is going to have, because it has been out there for a decade.

Does the observable harm justify heavy-handed censorship, the only kind that might work? The question is important because of the phenomenal awkwardness and far-reaching consequences of trying to do anything about Internet porn. How do you make illegal on the Web porn that is legally sold in dirty-book stores? How do you block content on servers in foreign countries? *Playboy* is a mainstream magazine with real literary content. To block on the Web content [that is] legal in the magazine makes no sense.

The Slippery Slope of Censorship

The real problem is this: To block the huge amount of "explicit content" on thousands of servers all over the world would require a massive federal bureaucracy of censors and lawyers and prosecutors. Anonymous and inaccessible bureaucrats would decide whether a nude painting by [the Spanish artist Francisco] Goya was porn. Unless the U.S. could force countries such as Japan and Thailand to outlaw what we regard as porn, all sorts of complex blocking of Internet service providers and domain names would be necessary.

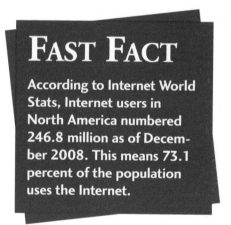

FAST FACT

According to Internet World Stats, Internet users in North America numbered 246.8 million as of December 2008. This means 73.1 percent of the population uses the Internet.

With this machinery in place, you can bet that censorship would be extended to "hate sites." This would come to mean any site the censors didn't like.

Goodbye Freedom of Expression

We can all guess with perfect accuracy what that would mean. One person's well-intentioned suggestions on a politically sensitive topic are another's hate. Goodbye freedom of expression.

An underlying truth is that many groups, including most governments, do not really like freedom of speech. Each will favor censorship for some admirable reason: preventing terrorism, political instability, moral decay, what have you. In sum: Do the purported benefits of reducing porn justify allowing government the power to incrementally dismember the First Amendment? You may think the government wouldn't abuse its powers.

The authors of the Bill of Rights were less sanguine.

EVALUATING THE AUTHORS' ARGUMENTS:

To make his argument that the Internet should not be censored, Fred Reed uses the example of pornography. In the previous viewpoint Peter Grad argues that the Internet should be censored by using the example of terrorism. Analyze the differences between these two examples. Does one seem more worthy of censorship than the other? Why or why not? Ultimately, do you think the Internet should be censored or not? Explain your reasoning.

Facts About Civil Liberties

Facts About Civil Liberties

Editor's note: These facts can be used in reports or papers to reinforce or add credibility when making important points or claims.

Civil Liberties and the Bill of Rights

Civil liberties in the United States are largely derived from the ten amendments that make up the Bill of Rights:

- The First Amendment: Congress shall make no law respecting an establishment of religion, or prohibiting the free exercise thereof; or abridging the freedom of speech or of the press; or the right of the people peaceably to assemble and to petition the government for a redress of grievances.

- The Second Amendment: A well-regulated militia, being necessary to the security of a free state, the right of the people to keep and bear arms shall not be infringed.

- The Third Amendment: No soldier shall, in time of peace, be quartered in any house without the consent of the owner, nor in time of war but in a manner to be prescribed by law.

- The Fourth Amendment: The right of the people to be secure in their persons, houses, papers, and effects, against unreasonable searches and seizures, shall not be violated, and no warrants shall issue but upon probable cause, supported by oath or affirmation, and particularly describing the place to be searched, and the persons or things to be seized.

- The Fifth Amendment: No person shall be held to answer for a capital or otherwise infamous crime unless on a presentment or indictment of a grand jury, except in cases arising in the land or naval forces, or in the militia, when in actual service, in time of war or public danger; nor shall any person be subject for the same offense to be twice put in jeopardy of life or limb; nor shall be compelled in any criminal case to be a witness against himself, nor be deprived of life, liberty, or property, without due process of law; nor shall private property be taken for public use without just compensation.

- The Sixth Amendment: In all criminal prosecutions, the accused shall enjoy the right to a speedy and public trial, by an impartial jury of the state and district wherein the crime shall have been committed, which districts shall have been previously ascertained by law, and to be informed of the nature and cause of the accusation; to be confronted with the witnesses against him; to have compulsory process for obtaining witnesses in his favor, and to have the assistance of counsel for his defense.
- The Seventh Amendment: In suits at common law, where the value in controversy shall exceed twenty dollars, the right of trial by jury shall be preserved, and no fact tried by a jury shall be otherwise reexamined in any court of the United States than according to the rules of the common law.
- The Eighth Amendment: Excessive bail shall not be required, nor excessive fines imposed, nor cruel and unusual punishments inflicted.
- The Ninth Amendment: The enumeration in the Constitution of certain rights shall not be construed to deny or disparage others retained by the people.
- The Tenth Amendment: The powers not delegated to the United States by the Constitution, nor prohibited by it to the states, are reserved to the states respectively, or to the people.

Civil Liberties and the First Amendment

According to the annual national State of the First Amendment Survey 2009:
- When asked to name the specific freedoms guaranteed by the First Amendment, 39 percent of Americans could not name any of the freedoms in the First Amendment.
- When asked about freedom of the press, 48 percent of Americans say the press has the right amount of freedom; 39 percent say it has too much freedom; and 7 percent say it has too little freedom.
- Two-thirds of Americans disagree with the assertion that the news media tries to report the news without bias.
- Seven in ten Americans say it is important for the news media to act as a watchdog on government.

The Obama Administration's Record on Civil Liberties

In 2006, as an Illinois senator, Barack Obama voted in favor of extending the PATRIOT Act.

During the first few days of his presidency Barack Obama made the following policy changes that pertain to civil liberties:

- January 22, 2009: Orders the closure of Guantánamo Bay detention facility.
- January 22, 2009: Bans the use of torture in order to promote the safe, lawful, and humane treatment of individuals in U.S. custody.
- January 23, 2009: Rescinds the Global Gag Rule, an antiabortion policy that detractors say undermines safe and effective family planning in developing countries.
- January 29, 2009: Signs the Lilly Ledbetter Fair Pay Restoration Act, which aims to move the United States closer to the goal of equal pay for equal work.

According to an August 2009 CNN/Opinion Research Poll:

- Forty-five percent of respondents disapprove of the way Barack Obama is handling the war on terror.
- Fifty-two percent approve of how Barack Obama is handling the war on terror.

Civil Liberties and the War on Terror

- A 2009 Pew Research study found that 75 percent of Republicans say it is acceptable for the government to monitor the communications of suspected terrorists without prior court permission. Fifty-six percent of Independents and 50 percent of Democrats view this policy as wrong.
- In 2009 a Pew Research study found that 42 percent of Republicans and Democrats believe that antiterrorism policies have not gone far enough to protect the country, while 36 percent say they have gone too far in restricting civil liberties.

Facts About Racial Profiling, Arab Americans, and Muslims

- A Pew Research Center study reported that 53 percent of Muslim Americans say it has become more difficult to be a Muslim in the United States since September 11, 2001. Most also believe that the government singles out Muslims for increased surveillance and monitoring.

According to Amnesty International USA:

- Forty-six states do not ban racial profiling based on religion or religious appearance.
- A 2004 Amnesty International USA study on racial profiling revealed that approximately 32 million Americans reported being victims of racial profiling. This is equivalent to the entire population of Canada.

According to a 2007 Zogby International Arab American Identity Study:

- 68 percent of Muslims think U.S. policies are disrespectful of Islam.
- 42 percent of Muslims have more pride in their heritage than they did ten years ago.
- 42 percent of Arab Americans have experienced discrimination based on ethnicity, while 58 percent of Arabs who identify themselves as Muslim have experienced discrimination.

According to a 2008 report released by the Council on American-Islamic Relations (CAIR):

- 2,652 civil rights complaints were made to CAIR in 2007.
- Eighty percent of Muslim civil rights abuses reported in 2007 occurred in nine states and the District of Columbia.
- Discrimination of Arabs and Muslims in the workplace increased by 18 percent from 2006 to 2007.

Civil Liberties and Internet Censorship

- According to the media rights group Reporters Without Borders, twelve nations have restricted their citizens from accessing online news and information deemed to be "undesirable": China, Burma, North Korea, Vietnam, Egypt, Iran, Syria, Saudi Arabia, Turkmenistan, Uzbekistan, Cuba, and Tunisia.

According to the New Media Institute:

- In January 2009 the Internet Watch Foundation reported that approximately three thousand Web sites contain child pornography.

Organizations to Contact

The editors have compiled the following list of organizations concerned with the issues debated in this book. The descriptions are derived from materials provided by the organizations. All have publications or information available for interested readers. The list was compiled on the date of publication of the present volume; the information provided here may change. Be aware that many organizations take several weeks or longer to respond to inquiries, so allow as much time as possible for the receipt of requested materials.

American-Arab Anti-Discrimination Committee (ADC)
1732 Wisconsin Ave. NW
Washington, DC 20007
(202) 244-2990
fax: (202) 244-7968
e-mail: webmaster@adc.org
Web site: www.adc.org

Founded in 1980, the ADC is an Arab American grassroots civil rights organization committed to defending the rights of people of Arab descent and promoting their cultural heritage. Through community advocacy it works to correct anti-Arab stereotypes found in the media, and through its Department of Legal Services it offers counseling in cases of discrimination and defamation. It issues the *ADC Times*, a bimonthly newsletter, issue papers, special reports, and action alerts, which call on members to advocate on behalf of the Arab American community.

American Civil Liberties Union (ACLU)
125 Broad St., 18th Fl.
New York, NY 10004-2400
(212) 549-2500
e-mail: aclu@aclu.org
Web site: www.aclu.org

The ACLU is a national organization that works to defend Americans' civil rights guaranteed by the U.S. Constitution. It argues daily in courts, legislatures, and communities to preserve individual liberties, such as freedom of speech, freedom of the press, and privacy rights. Following the September 2001 terrorist attacks, the ACLU founded its National Security Project, which litigates national security cases involving discrimination, torture, detention, surveillance, and secrecy, to protect every human's fundamental rights.

Center for Campus Free Speech
407 S. Dearborn, Ste. 701
Chicago, IL 60605
(312) 291-0396
e-mail: center@campusspeech.org
Web site: www.campusspeech.org

The Center for Campus Free Speech is a coalition of students, faculty, administrators, and others working to protect and promote free speech on university campuses. The center provides specialized support to campuses and creates a national network for concerned educators, administrators, lawyers, and students. It also spearheads several projects focused on student civil rights, academic freedom, free speech zones, and what it views as restrictive campus speech codes. Guides, fact sheets, toolkits, and reports—including *Campus Voices*, a report that finds that education works best with a free exchange of ideas—can be located on its Web site.

Council on American-Islamic Relations (CAIR)
453 New Jersey Ave. SE
Washington, DC 20003
(202) 488-8787
fax: (202) 488-0833
e-mail: info@cair.com
Web site: www.cair.com

CAIR is a nonprofit Muslim civil liberties and advocacy group that works to enhance understanding of Islam, encourages dialogue, protects civil liberties, promotes justice, and empowers American Muslims.

Press releases, action alerts, and legislation concerning Muslim American civil liberties can all be found on CAIR's Web site. It also produces an annual civil rights report that explores issues facing the Muslim American community, including a 2008 annual report on Muslim American civil rights entitled *The Status of Muslim Civil Rights in the United States 2008: Without Fear of Discrimination.*

Electronic Frontier Foundation (EFF)
454 Shotwell St.
San Francisco, CA 94110-1914
(415) 436-9333
fax: (415) 436-9993
e-mail: information@eff.org
Web site: www.eff.org

Founded in 1990, the EFF is a nonprofit watchdog organization that defends civil liberties on the Internet. The EFF blends the expertise of policy analysts, lawyers, technologists, and activists to confront threats to free speech, privacy, innovation, intellectual property, and consumer rights in the digital world. It produces a number of white papers on privacy and the Internet, all of which are available through its Web site.

Human Rights Watch
350 Fifth Ave., 34th Fl.
New York, NY 10118-3299
(212) 290-4700
fax: (212) 736-1300
e-mail: hrwnyc@hrw.org
Web site: www.hrw.org

Human Rights Watch is an independent organization that regularly investigates human rights abuses in over seventy countries around the world and holds violators of these rights accountable. It works to lay the legal and moral groundwork to defend and protect human rights for all while also promoting civil liberties and defending freedom of thought, due process, and equal protection of the law. It publishes the *Human Rights Watch Quarterly Newsletter* and the annual *Human Rights Watch World Report.*

Institute for Justice
901 North Glebe Rd., Ste. 900
Arlington, VA 22203
(703) 682-9320
fax: (703) 682-9321
e-mail: general@ij.org
Web site: www.ij.org

The Institute for Justice is a libertarian public interest law firm providing litigation and advocacy on behalf of individuals whose most basic rights have been violated by the government. It works to secure economic liberty, private property rights, and freedom of speech for all members of society, and it aims to restore constitutional limits on the power of government. Some of its publications include *Liberty & Law*, a bimonthly newsletter, various reports, articles, and papers on various liberty interests.

National Coalition Against Censorship (NCAC)
275 Seventh Ave., Ste. 1504
New York, NY 10001
(212) 807-6222
fax: (212) 807-6245
e-mail: ncac@ncac.org
Web site: www.ncac.org

The NCAC is an alliance of fifty national nonprofit organizations committed to protecting First Amendment rights though both local and national public education and advocacy. The coalition has several projects dedicated to protecting freedom of expression and the public's right to receive accurate and truthful information, including The Knowledge Project: Censorship and Science and The Youth Free Expression Network. It also publishes *Censorship News*, a quarterly newsletter, and other reports.

U.S. Department of Homeland Security
Washington, DC 20528
(202) 282-8000
Web site: www.dhs.gov

The DHS was created after the September 11, 2001, terrorist attacks. The department serves to secure the nation while preserving American freedoms and liberties. It is charged with protecting the United States from terrorists, decreasing the country's vulnerability to terrorism, and effectively responding to attacks. The current DHS homeland security strategic plan can be found on its Web site.

U.S. Department of Justice (DOJ)
950 Pennsylvania Ave. NW
Washington, DC 20530-0001
(202) 514-2000
e-mail: AskDOJ@usdoj.gov
Web site: www.usdoj.gov

The DOJ functions to enforce the law and defend the interests of the United States. Its primary duties are to ensure public safety against foreign and domestic threats; to provide federal leadership in preventing and controlling crime; to seek just punishment for those guilty of unlawful behavior; to administer and enforce the nation's immigration laws fairly and effectively; and to ensure fair and impartial administration of justice for all Americans.

For Further Reading

Books

Bamford, James. *The Shadow Factory: The NSA from 9/11 to the Eaves-dropping on America.* New York: Anchor, 2009. Argues that the National Security Agency failed to protect Americans from the 9/11 terrorist attacks and examines how its mistakes led to a dramatic increase in domestic surveillance of innocent citizens.

Cateur, Linda. *Voices of American Muslims: 23 Profiles.* New York: Hippocrene 2009. Profiles the lives of twenty-three American Muslims from all walks of life through first-person narratives.

Davis, Darren W. *Negative Liberty: Public Opinion and the Terrorist Attacks on America.* New York: Russell Sage Foundation, 2009. Examines Americans' perceptions of the relationship between national security and civil liberties after the 9/11 terrorist attacks.

Dupree, Anne Profitt. *Speaking Up: The Unintended Cost of Free Speech in Public Schools.* Cambridge, MA: Harvard University Press, 2009. Explores multiple court cases related to free speech in public education to illustrate the tension between a school's desire to maintain a safe learning environment and a student's desire to explore the boundaries of free speech.

Grayling, A.C. *Liberty in the Age of Terror: A Defence of Civil Society and Enlightenment Values.* London: Bloomsbury, 2010. Argues that Western governments often restrict their own citizens' civil liberties when they start wars in the name of defending freedom and democracy from terrorism.

Kaminer, Wendy. *Worst Instincts: Cowardice, Conformity, and the ACLU.* Boston: Beacon, 2009. Discusses the author's disillusionment with the American Civil Liberties Union as it has shifted its focus away from the founding principles of freedom of expression, due process, and the rights of individuals and has, instead, adopted a herd mentality.

Nunziato, Dawn C. *Virtual Freedom: Net Neutrality and Free Speech in the Internet Age.* Stanford, CA: Stanford University Press, 2009.

Examines the state of free speech on the Internet and how Internet censorship threatens Americans' right to freedom of expression.

O'Leary, Brad. *Shut Up America! The End of Free Speech*. New York: WND, 2009. Argues that America's liberal politicians threaten citizens' First Amendment right to free speech and that censorship in America is gaining momentum under President Barack Obama's administration.

Romero, Anthony, and Dina Temple-Raston. *In Defense of Our America: The Fight for Civil Liberties in the Age of Terror.* New York: William Morrow, 2007. Provides behind-the-scenes accounts of people who have experienced civil liberties violations in post-9/11 America.

Shiell, Timothy C. *Campus Hate Speech on Trial.* Lawrence: University Press of Kansas, 2009. Analyzes the conflict between the need to ensure free speech on college campuses, while limiting racist and sexist speech.

Periodicals and Internet Sources

Baer, Merrit. "Will We Put Guantánamo Detainees on Trial for Terrorist Speech?" GlobalComment, July 1, 2009. http://globalcomment.com/2009/will-we-put-guantanamo-detainees-on-trial-for-terrorist-speech.

Benson, Pam. "'Enhanced Interrogations' Don't Work, Ex-FBI Agent Tells Panel," CNN, May 13, 2009. www.edition.cnn.com/2009/POLITICS/05/13/interrogation.hearing/index.html.

Duvvuru, Kamalakar. "'Your Name Is Common': Racial Profiling in the US," Dissident Voice, August 22, 2009. http://dissidentvoice.org/2009/08/%E2%80%9Cyour-name-is-common%E2%80%9D-racial-profiling-in-the-us.

Emery, Aaron. "Water Boarding and the Future State of Torture," Campaign for Liberty, July 3, 2009. www.campaignforliberty.com/article.php?view=110.

Eugene (OR) Register-Guard. "Censoring the Internet," July 2, 2008.

Frum, David. "Flying Blind: Airport Screeners Treat Everyone the Same. They Shouldn't," American Enterprise Institute, August 12, 2006. www.aei.org/article/24777.

Grand Junction (CO) Daily Sentinel. "Parents Must Filter Internet, Not Censors," May 1, 2008.

Greenberg, Karen J. "8 Reasons to Close Guantánamo Now," *In These Times*, February 12, 2007.

Halperin, Morton H. "Listening to Compromise," *New York Times*, July 8, 2008.

Hansen, Jonathan. "Don't Close Gitmo," *Guardian* (London), June 2, 2009.

Heins, Marjorie, Christina Cho, and Ariel Feldman. "Internet Filters: A Public Policy Report," Brennan Center for Justice, 2006. www.fepproject.org/policyreports/filters2.pdf.

Levy, Janet. "One-Way Free Speech," *American Thinker*, July 20, 2009.

Liptak, Adam. "Hate Speech or Free Speech? What Much of West Bans Is Protected in U.S.," *International Herald Tribune*, June 11, 2008.

McCarthy, Andrew C. "Why Close Gitmo? Its Critics Will Never Be Satisfied," *National Review*, February 25, 2009.

Melber, Ari. "Will Democrats Restore Our Liberties Stolen in the Bush Era?" AlterNet, November 10, 2007. www.alternet.org/rights/67488/?page=1.

Morozov, Evgeny. "To Stop Dissent, Call It Smut," *Newsweek International*, February 2, 2009.

Murdock, Deroy. "Waterboarding Has Its Benefits," *National Review*, November 5, 2007.

Prieto, Daniel B. "War About Terror: Civil Liberties and National Security After 9/11," Council on Foreign Relations, February 2009. www.cfr.org/publication/18373.

Reed, Fred. "Slippery Slope of a Web Censor," *Washington Times*, October 27, 2007.

Rosen, Jeffrey. "Free Speech on the Web: Is the Internet Really the Bastion of Free Expression That We Think It Is?" *New York Times Upfront*, January 12, 2009.

Serwer, Adam. "Report Card on Civil Liberties," *American Prospect*, April 15, 2009.

Soufan, Ali. "My Tortured Decision," *New York Times*, April 22, 2009.

Soupcoff, Marni. "Mark Freiman Makes the Case for Censoring Hate," *National Post*, May 21, 2008.

Street-Porter, Janet. "We Must Rescue Boys from Cyberspace So They Can Live in the Real World," *Independent on Sunday* (London), June 24, 2007.

Thompson, Bill. "Which Freedoms Do We Want Online?" BBC,

May 23, 2007. http://news.bbc.co.uk/2/hi/technology/6685253
.stm.

Tomlinson, Herschel. "BORDC Grades Obama on Privacy and Civil
Liberties," *Dallas (TX) Progressive Examiner,* September 29, 2009.

Trent, Brian. "National ID Card Threatens Security," PopulistAmer-
ica, April 15, 2007. www.populistamerica.com/national_id_card_
threatens_security.

Yoo, John. "Why We Endorsed Warrantless Wiretaps," *Wall Street Journal,* July 16, 2009.

Web Sites

ACLU's National Security Project (www.aclu.org/natsec/gen/
38798res20090224.html). Created by the American Civil Liberties Union, the National Security Project (NSP) advocates for national security policies that are consistent with the Constitution,
the rule of law, and fundamental human rights.

The Independent Institute (www.independent.org). The Independent Institute is a nonpartisan independent organization dedicated
to the scholarly inquiry of a number of public policy issues. The
Institute sponsors six educational centers, including the Center on
Law and Justice, which works toward meaningful legal reform in
areas of criminal justice, constitutional law, property rights, and
civil liberties.

The Investigative Project on Terrorism (www.investigativeproject
.org). This independent nonprofit research group has compiled the
world's most comprehensive data center on radical Islamic terrorist groups. Its Web site provides critical information on the opera-
tions, funding, and activities of Islamic terrorist groups in the United
States and around the world.

New America Media (http://news.newamericamedia.org). New America Media (NAM) is America's largest national collaboration and
advocate of two thousand ethnic news organizations. The agency
is dedicated to bringing the voices of ethnic minorities, immigrants,
young people, and the elderly into the national discourse.

OpenNet Initiative (www.opennet.net). A collaborative partnership
of four leading academic institutions, OpenNet aims to investigate,
expose, and analyze Internet filtering and surveillance practices to
inform public policy and advocacy work.

People for the American Way (www.pfaw.org). This organization is committed to reaffirming the traditional American values of equality, diversity, and freedom of expression. It aims to cultivate new generations of leaders and activists who will sustain these critical civil liberties and create a climate of tolerance and respect for all people.

Rights Working Group (www.rightsworkinggroup.org). A national coalition of civil liberties, national security, and human rights organizations, the Rights Working Group is committed to restoring due process and human rights protections that have been eroded in the aftermath of the terror attacks on September 11.

Index

Picture Credits

Alaska Airline/Getty Images, 62
AP Images, 13, 21, 42, 55, 79, 98, 109
Dennis Brack/Landov, 103
Kevin Dietsch/UPI/Landov, 48, 67, 115
Bill Greenblatt/UPI/Landov, 73
Zahid Hussein/Reuters/Landov, 88
© kleo67/Alamy, 51
Luke MacGregor/Reuters/Landov, 84
Patrick D. McDermott/UPI/Landov, 28
Ian Nicholson/PA Photos/Landov, 92
Jason Reed/Reuters/Landov, 35
Reuters/Landov, 10
Steve Zmina, 16, 22, 30, 40, 56–57, 63, 68, 74, 86, 91, 96, 111, 117, 121